CERTAIN CONCERNS
for the Christian Life

ANDREW LANSDOWN

Certain Concerns for the Christian Life

© Andrew Lansdown 2021

ISBN: 978-1-76111-057-3

Published by Rhiza Press
P. O. Box 302
Chinchilla QLD 4413
Australia
www.wombatrhiza.com.au

Cover and layout by Rhiza Press

A catalogue record for this
book is available from the
National Library of Australia

For Dwight Randall, fellow labourer and friend

We destroy arguments
and every proud obstacle to the knowledge of God,
and take every thought captive to obey Christ ...
2 Corinthians 10:5 (RSV)

Contents

Gospel Concerns

Becoming a Christian

The Christian faith is based on a belief that there is a true and living God who is good and great. By his wisdom and power, God made everything, including human beings, whom he created in his own image. God loves human beings, and he communicates openly with them through his word, the Bible.

A Christian is a person who has a close, personal relationship with this God who created us and loves us. But how can someone enter into such a relationship? Or to put it another way, how can someone become a Christian?

Our dilemma

The Bible teaches that our relationship with God has been ruined because of our sins, our wrongdoings. "Your iniquities have made a separation between you and your God, and your sins have hid his face from you" (Isa 59:2). Because he is morally pure (holy), God cannot and will not tolerate wrong of any sort.

Sadly, all people are alienated from God, because "all have sinned and fall short of the glory of God" (Rom 3:23). Every one of us has said and done and thought things that are wrong, things that fall short of God's perfect character and holy standards. Although we may be innocent of sins like murder, robbery and adultery, we are guilty of the sins (hatred, envy and lust) that give rise to them. In varying degrees, our attitudes and actions are spoiled by sins such as pride, resentment, selfishness, and dishonesty. "None is righteous"—that is, virtuous, morally right—"no, not one" (Rom 3:10).

We are wrongdoers. Worse still, even our attempts to do good have failed dismally. "All our righteous deeds are like a polluted garment" (Isa 64:6). Try as we might, we cannot free our lives from the taint of sin. So we cannot make amends to God and come back into a right relationship with him by our own efforts.

And as if our sinfulness and our helplessness were not bad enough, the Bible declares that "the wages of sin is death" (Rom 6:23). The wage, the just payment, for our wrongdoing is to be condemned for eternity to a living death in hell. Jesus warns that nothing could be worse than "to go to hell, to the unquenchable fire" (Mark 9:43).

This, then, is our dilemma. We are sinful. God is holy. Because of what we are and what God is, we are separated from God. This separation means eternal punishment for us. And we can do nothing about it, because even our best efforts fall far short of God's perfect standards.

God's solution

But thankfully, this is not where the matter ends. For while God hates sin, he loves sinners. He is angry with us, yet he still loves us. So he implemented a plan to save us. He "sent the Son into the world ... that the world might be saved through him" (John 3:17). And the Son whom he sent is Jesus.

The Lord Jesus Christ is God's only Son, and he "came into the world to save sinners" (1 Tim 1:15). Jesus himself said that he "came to seek and to save the lost" (Luke 19:10).

To save us from God's anger, Jesus had to remove our sins. And to do this he had to forfeit his life, for the Bible says that "without the shedding of blood there is no forgiveness of sins" (Heb 9:22). Sin must be punished, and the punishment is death. There is no way around this. If God simply let us off, it would make a mockery of his justice and his holiness. So to enable God to extend his love without offending his justice, Jesus willingly came to die for us.

Jesus became our substitute. He offered himself as a sacrifice to God for us. "He himself bore our sins in his body on the cross" (1 Pet 2:24). And along with our sins, Jesus bore our punishment. "He was wounded for our transgressions ... upon him was the chastisement that made us whole" (Isa 53:5).

On the cross at Calvary Jesus made an exchange. He died in our place and on our behalf. He bore our sins so that we might bear his righteousness and he suffered our punishment so that we might enjoy his reward.

The good news of the Christian faith is this: "God shows his love for us in that while we were yet sinners Christ died for us" (Rom 5:8). "For the wages of sin is death, but the free gift of God is eternal life in Christ Jesus our Lord" (Rom 6:23).

Eternal life is a gift, God's gift to sinners. We do not deserve it. We cannot earn it. We can only receive it.

But how? How can we take hold of this gift?

Our response

We receive the gift of salvation by personally believing in Jesus as our Lord and Saviour. A man once asked Jesus' followers, "What must I do to be saved?" They replied, "Believe in the Lord Jesus, and you will be saved" (Acts 16:30-31). So then, "if you confess with your lips that Jesus is Lord and believe in your heart that God raised him from the dead, you will be saved" (Rom 10:9).

Jesus himself said, "I am the resurrection and the life; he who believes in me, though he die, yet shall he live" (John 11:25). Again he said, "I have come as light into the world, that whoever believes in me may not remain in darkness" (John 12:46).

The Bible commonly refers to Christians as "believers". This name defines not only what Christians are, but also how they came to be that way.

But what exactly does the Bible mean when it commands us to "believe" in Jesus?

Belief (or faith) in Jesus involves agreement. We must agree with what the Bible says about him. We must believe that he is the Son of God, that he was born of the virgin Mary, that he lived a sinless life, that he died on the cross for our sins, that he rose bodily from the dead, and that he lives and reigns forevermore.

Belief in Jesus also involves repentance. With deep sorrow and regret, we must own up to the fact that we are sinners. We must admit our wrongdoing to him and ask him for forgiveness. Repentance also involves a change of attitude. It is not enough to confess our sins and to feel sorry about them. We must determine, with God's help, to abandon our sinful ways.

Belief in Jesus also involves submission. We cannot accept him as Saviour without also accepting him as Lord. This means that we must be prepared to give him control of our lives. We must be prepared to follow his lead and to yield to his will.

Belief in Jesus also involves love. We are not embracing an abstract philosophy but a living person. By faith, we are entering into a loving relationship with him.

4

When we believe in Jesus, we trust him to save us and rely on him to lead us in "the paths of righteousness" (Ps 23:3). We commit ourselves to him and he becomes "the Shepherd and Guardian of our souls" (1 Pet 2:25). And then we find ourselves saying with humility and wonder, "I know Jesus loves me, and I love him back!"

It is difficult for us to accept that we do not have to earn our salvation in some way. The people of Jesus' time had the same difficulty. They asked him, "What must we do, to be doing the works of God?" They were thinking of good deeds and religious rituals. But Jesus answered them, "This is the work of God, that you believe in him whom he sent" (John 6:28-29).

God wants us to believe in Jesus—nothing more, nothing less. And when we do, he saves us and enters into a loving Father-child relationship with us.

The Bible emphasises that good deeds and religious rituals have no part to play in our salvation. Indeed, "a man is not justified by works of the law but through faith in Jesus Christ" (Gal 2:16). God does not say, "I will save you if you are good." He says, "I will save you if you trust in my Son—and then I will make you good!"

Stressing that salvation comes by the grace of God through faith in Christ and not by anything we can do, the Bible states: "if justification were through the law, then Christ died to no purpose" (Gal 2:21). If we could be saved by our own efforts to obey God's moral law, then Christ would not have needed to die for us. His sacrifice would have been pointless.

Our only way

Some people believe that there are many ways to approach God and so attain eternal life. But the Bible insists that there is only one way, and that way is Jesus. "There is salvation in no one else, for there is no other name under heaven given among men by which we must be saved" (Acts 4:12). Jesus himself insists, "he who rejects me rejects him who sent me" (Luke 10:16).

Some people claim that it is arrogant to insist that Jesus is the only one who can save us. In fact, the reverse is true. The ultimate arrogance is to think that we know better than Jesus does. The ultimate humility is to agree with Jesus when he says, "I am the way, and the truth, and the life; no one comes to the Father, but by me" (John 14:6).

Other people claim that Christians are exclusivists because they insist that Jesus is the only one who can reconcile us to God and bring us to heaven. This, too, is untrue. For Christians invite all people to believe in Jesus and be saved. They say to all people, "God loves you. Christ died for you. Believe in him and be saved with us!" This is not exclusive but inclusive, if only people are willing to be included.

While it is true that many people will be excluded from eternal life, this is by their own choice. As Jesus said to some of the religious leaders of his day, "you refuse to come to me that you may have life" (John 5:40).

Our heartfelt request

God "desires all men to be saved" (1 Tim 2:4). Jesus "gave himself as a ransom for all" (1 Tim 2:6). Consequently, "whoever calls on the name of the Lord shall be saved" (Acts 2:21).

We can call to Jesus in prayer. Whatever the time, wherever the place, Jesus hears us when we speak to him, and he graciously responds to our requests.

To become a Christian—to be reconciled to God, to receive the gift of salvation—a person must sincerely and humbly pray along these lines:

> Jesus, I believe that you are the sinless Son of God, the Saviour of the world, the risen Lord. I believe that you died on the cross for me, and I thank you for it. I confess my sins to you with shame and sadness, and I renounce them. I ask you to forgive me. I ask you to come into my life to be my own Saviour and Lord. I trust you. Help me to love, worship and obey you.

This is the first prayer of every believer. An earnest desire to pray such a prayer is proof that God is working in a person's heart to bring that person into his eternal kingdom.

God's blessings

When we personally believe in Jesus as our Lord and Saviour, many wonderful things happen. Our sins are forgiven and we are made clean in the sight of God (1 Cor 6:9-11). We are saved from the punishment we deserve because of our sin (Rom 5:9; 8:1). We become the children of God (John 1:12). We receive eternal life (John 3:15; 5:24). We begin to understand the purpose of life (1 Pet 2:9). We begin to experience "the peace of God, which passes all understanding" (Phil 4:7). These are some of the things that happen to and in and with us when we become Christians.

One other change deserves a special mention. When we believe in Jesus, the Spirit of God comes to live within us forever (John 14:16-17). It is the Holy Spirit, the Spirit of Christ, who pours God's love into our hearts (Rom 5:5), seals us as God's possession (Eph 1:13-14; 4:30), assures us that we are God's children (Rom 8:14-17), and changes us day by day into the likeness of the Lord Jesus (2 Cor 3:18).

Our responsibilities

While God requires nothing of us except faith before our salvation, afterwards he requires a great deal. And it is the Holy Spirit who gives us both the desire and the power to meet these requirements.

As Christians, we should regularly read God's word, the Bible, asking God to help us to understand, believe and obey it. We might begin with the Gospels of Matthew, Mark, Luke and John, but we will not stop there. We will read every page of the Bible, meditating on what we read and memorising important passages.

As Christians, we should speak with God regularly in prayer. He is our Father, so we can approach him with familiarity and affection. He is also our Sovereign, so we should approach him with reverence and respect. In the name of Jesus and by the power of the Holy Spirit, we should talk to our Father often.

As Christians, we should worship together with other Christian people. We need to find a church where the Bible is fully believed and taught, then commit ourselves to attend the services each Sunday, making the church our spiritual home.

As Christians, we should be baptised. Jesus himself was baptised and we are commanded to follow his example. Baptism symbolises our union with Christ in his death, burial and resurrection. It is an outward expression of our inward conversion, and offers us the opportunity to publicly declare our allegiance to Jesus as Lord.

As Christians, we should strive to live lives that are holy and good. Now that we are saved, we want to live in a manner that is fitting to our salvation.

If we heed them, the Bible, the Holy Spirit and our consciences will help us to live in a way that is clean towards God and kind towards others. The Lord Jesus summarised our spiritual and social responsibilities as Christians in this way: "You shall love the Lord your God with all your heart, and with all your soul, and with all your mind. This is the great and first commandment. And a second is like it, You shall love your neighbour as yourself" (Matt 22:37-39).

And finally, as Christians, we should share our faith with others so that they, too, might be saved. We want everyone to hear the good news that "God so loved the world that he gave his only Son, that whoever believes in him should not perish but have eternal life" (John 3:16).

One for All

Christianity is an inclusive religion. In the fundamental matters of origin, nature, worth, sin and judgment, the Christian faith includes everyone in the same category. It maintains that: all people have been created by God; all people bear the image of God; all people are precious to God; all people have done things that are wrong in God's eyes; and all people face God's judgment because of their wrongdoing. In all these matters, Christianity makes no distinction or exclusion on the basis of ethnicity, gender, class or colour.

The Christian faith is particularly concerned with the universal predicament of mankind. And the predicament is not only that all people are sinners and consequently under threat of judgment—it is also that all people are helpless and consequently in need of a Saviour.

The Christian solution to the human predicament is called the "gospel", the "good news". And the gospel can be summarised in this way: *God desires all people to be saved, and so he sent his Son to be the Saviour of the world, so that everyone who believes in him will be saved.* Each part of this summary accords with God's word, the Bible, and is worthy of further consideration.

God's inclusive desire

The first part of Christianity's good news involves God's yearning for the eternal welfare of all people. Many passages in the Bible highlight God's all-inclusive desire:

- God himself urges, "Turn to me and be saved, all you ends of the earth" (Isa 45:22).*
- God also declares, "I take no pleasure in the death of anyone ... Repent and live!" (Ezek 18:32).

- Again God declares, "I take no pleasure in the death of the wicked, but rather that they turn from their ways and live. Turn! Turn from your evil ways!" (Ezek 33:11).
- The apostle Paul states, "God our Saviour ... wants all men to be saved and to come to a knowledge of the truth" (1 Tim 2:4).
- The apostle Peter states, "The Lord ... is patient with you, not wanting anyone to perish, but everyone to come to repentance" (2 Pet 3:9).

No one is excluded from God's desire to save sinners. He wants all people to turn to him so that they might enjoy eternal life.

God's inclusive provision

God loves all people and desires their salvation. But this is not where the matter ends. God did not merely desire our eternal welfare and then do nothing about it. On the contrary, he sent his own Son, Jesus, to make amends for our sins by his death on the cross.

The second part of the Christian good news, then, is that in Jesus God has provided a Saviour for all people everywhere. Again, many passages in the Bible highlight God's all-inclusive provision:

- The prophet Isaiah says of Jesus, "the LORD has laid on him the iniquity of us all" (Isa 53:6).
- John the Baptist says of Jesus, "Look, the Lamb of God, who takes away the sin of the world!" (John 1:29).
- Paul says of Jesus, "we are convinced that one died for all ... he died for all" (2 Cor 5:14-15).
- Paul also says that Jesus "gave himself as a ransom for all men" (1 Tim 2:6).
- Again Paul says that Jesus became a man "so that by the grace of God he might taste death for everyone" (Heb 2:9).
- The apostle John says, "He is the atoning sacrifice for our sins, and not only for ours but also for the sins of the whole world" (1 John 2:2).
- John also says, "the Father has sent his Son to be the Saviour of the world" (1 John 4:14).

No one is excluded from God's provision for sinners. He sent Jesus to die for the sins of everyone.

God's inclusive invitation

God desires all to be saved, and to that end he sent his Son to be the Saviour of all. Yet salvation is not automatically given to anyone, but must be personally accepted by faith. To encourage this, God extends an invitation to all people to have faith in his Son.

The third part of the Christian good news, then, is that God invites everyone to come to Jesus to be saved. Again, many passages in the Bible highlight God's all-inclusive invitation:

- The Lord Jesus himself declares, "God so loved the world that he gave his one and only Son, that whoever believes in him shall not perish but have eternal life" (John 3:16).
- Jesus invites, "Come to me, all you who are weary and burdened, and I will give you rest" (Matt 11:28).
- Peter says, "Everyone who calls on the name of the Lord will be saved" (Acts 2:21).
- Peter also says, "everyone who believes in him receives forgiveness of sins through his name" (Acts 10:43).
- Paul says, "if you confess with your mouth, 'Jesus is Lord,' and believe in your heart that God raised him from the dead, you will be saved. ... As the Scripture says, 'Anyone who trusts in him will never be put to shame.' For there is no difference between Jew and Gentile—the same Lord is Lord of all and richly blesses all who call on him, for, 'Everyone who calls on the name of the Lord will be saved'" (Rom 10:9-13).
- John says, "Whoever is thirsty, let him come; and whoever wishes, let him take the free gift of the water of life" (Rev 22:17).

No one is excluded from God's invitation to come to Jesus as Saviour. Everyone is invited, and those who respond in repentance and faith are assured of forgiveness of sins, rest for their souls and eternal life.

God's exclusive way

God invites all people to trust in his Son as their Saviour. Those who accept God's invitation will be saved. Those who reject his invitation will not be saved. The inclusiveness of Christianity unavoidably turns to exclusiveness at this point.

Jesus is unique. He alone has done all that God requires for our salvation, so he alone can save us. Many passages in the Bible highlight the uniqueness of Jesus as Saviour and reveal him to be the exclusive way to God:

- Jesus himself declares, "I am the way and the truth and the life. No one comes to the Father except through me" (John 14:6).
- Jesus also says, "he who rejects me rejects him who sent me" (Luke 10:16).
- Peter says, "Salvation is found in no one else, for there is no other name under heaven given to men by which we must be saved" (Acts 4:12).
- Paul says, "there is one God and one mediator between God and men, the man Christ Jesus" (1 Tim 2:5).
- John says, "No one who denies the Son has the Father; whoever acknowledges the Son has the Father also" (1 John 2:23).
- John also says, "God has given us eternal life, and this life is in his Son. He who has the Son has life; he who does not have the Son of God does not have life" (1 John 5:11-12).

According to the plain teaching of the Bible, only Jesus can save us from judgment and reconcile us to God. In all the earth there is no other name to call upon for salvation.

Some people take offence at the Christian claim that Jesus is *the only one*. But why should they, since he is the only one *for everyone*? None are excluded—none except those who exclude themselves by refusing to come to Jesus that they might have life.

Since God sent Jesus to be the Saviour of all people, it is perfectly reasonable that he requires all people to trust in Jesus to be saved. *One for all* is God's provision: *all for one* is his proviso.

Conclusion

God desires all people to be saved, and so he sent his Son to be the Saviour of the world, so that everyone who believes in him will be saved. This is the good news, the gospel of hope at the heart of the Christian faith.

And it is good news for everyone. God has no favourites. He sent one for all. And that one is Jesus.

Sticky Tape Mechanic

While driving along a country road one evening, I passed a car that appeared to have broken down. Seeing a figure stooped in the headlights, I pulled over to offer assistance.

The driver was a young man with shoulder-length hair—almost as long as I once had my own. It was evident from the board that took up most of the room in his small car that he was a surfer.

He was bent over a headlight, doing something to it. When he straightened up to speak to me, I noticed that he had a roll of sticky-tape in his hand—ordinary, thin, transparent, flimsy sticky-tape!

I asked him what was wrong.

"Oh, I swerved to miss a 'roo the other day and hit a pole," he said, pointing to the left mudguard, which was stoved in. "And now this headlight," he said, pointing to the right one, "keeps dropping down. I can't see the road properly, so I'm trying to lift it up."

It was a sorry looking car and, as far as I could see, *both* headlights were droopy-eyed and looked as if they were about to nod off forever. And here was this young man trying to fix one of them with sticky tape!

He thanked me for stopping but said he didn't think there was anything I could do. And he was right. Short of helping him to abandon the old bomb, there was nothing I could do. So, I left him there on the roadside with his drooping headlights and his sticky tape.

For several days after, I found myself wondering how he got on. I know that even if he managed to fix his vehicle with the sticky tape, the repair would not have lasted long.

What this young surfer was doing with his car is a picture of what many of us do with our lives. Our lives are ruined by sin, but we try to mend them with the flimsy tape of good works or religious practices. We try, but the task is hopeless.

What we sinners need is not *mended* lives but *new* lives. The Lord Jesus Christ came to earth to meet this need. He died for our sins so that God could do what he promised through the prophet Ezekiel: "A new heart I will give you, and a new spirit I will put within you; and I will take out of your flesh the heart of stone and give you a heart of flesh. And I will put my Spirit within you …" (36:26).

God is no sticky tape mechanic. He knows the main problem with us is that we have stony hearts—hearts that are insensitive to his goodness and hostile to his holiness. He knows this radical problem requires a radical solution—the replacement of a tough with a tender heart. And he provided that solution through his pure-, brave-, tender-hearted Son.

So, when we repent of our sins and commit ourselves by faith to Jesus, God gives us a new heart. Or to put it another way, he instils in our nature a radically new attitude towards himself. Before conversion we have a hard and rebellious heart, a heart of stone; but after conversion we have a soft and responsive heart, a heart of flesh. Our mind and will and emotions are altered in relation to him.

This alteration comes about because God sends his Holy Spirit to live within us. Of course, his Spirit does not replace our spirit, for then we would cease to be human and become divine. Rather, God's Spirit bears witness with our spirit that we now stand in a new relationship to God—for he has become our Father, and we his children (Rom 8:16). And his Spirit works in partnership with our spirit to regulate our desires and thoughts and conduct. By implanting his Spirit within us, God transforms our desires and empowers us to live according to his will.

Every person needs a new relationship with God, a new attitude towards God, a new desire to please God, a new power to obey God, a new Spirit to be morally like God. On the cross at Calvary, Jesus made provision for these needs; and his provision is effective for all who will receive it by faith.

An Accurate Diagnosis

A man collapsed on the street with severe chest pains. A doctor chanced upon him, took him to hospital, and ran various tests.

"I'm sorry to have to tell you this," the doctor said at last, "but you are very sick. You have cancer, lung cancer."

The man reached into his pocket for a cigarette to calm his nerves. After lighting up, he said to the doctor, "Who do you think you are, telling me I've got cancer? I don't have to take that sort of talk from you!"

"Look," the doctor replied, "the cancer is at a relatively early stage. I've seen worse. There's still hope for you, if you'll give up smoking and submit to treatment."

"Ah, I see," said the man. "You not only want to put me down, you also want to control me. First you tell me I'm *sick* and next you tell me I have to *submit* to you *or else!*" He took a drag on his cigarette, coughed, and continued: "You're a typical doctor—always so negative, telling people they've got diseases. And you're so high and mighty, too, threatening people with death if they don't do as you say."

"No," the doctor interrupted. "You don't understand. You're seriously ill and if—"

But the man would not listen. "I understand all right," he said, "and you can get lost as far as I'm concerned! I'm not going to let anyone humiliate me by telling me I'm sick. And I'm not going to let anyone scare me by telling me I'm going to die. And I'm sure not going to let anyone tell me what I have to do!"

Sound absurd? Don't be too sure.

It is true that few people behave like that sick man concerning their physical health. But when it comes to their spiritual health, many people behave precisely like him.

15

God's word, the Bible, claims that all human beings are afflicted with a moral disorder, a spiritual sickness, called "sinfulness". Humans are sinful, having a nature that is stained by evil and biased towards doing wrong. Many people find this claim deeply offensive. They feel that it demeans humanity, and therefore themselves. They take it as a personal put-down.

But try for a moment to set aside the seeming affront of being described as a sinner, and think soberly about the human condition. Whichever way we look at it, there is something fundamentally wrong with human beings.

We sense this quite clearly when we repeatedly read in the newspapers about people who have done dreadful things—people guilty of murder, rape, abuse, burglary, bashing, robbery, embezzlement, bigotry, adultery and deception. Even with the best will in the world, even with the most ingenious theories about the influences of poverty or parents, we cannot quite escape the conviction that the problem with such people lies in their hearts. We cannot shake the thought that the evil they commit has to do with the evil they harbour.

It is not just strangers, however, who alert us to the fact that humans have a moral problem. Although we hate to admit it, we observe a similar problem in those close to us, those we love. Our children, for example. Of course, they have not robbed or bashed anyone—at least, not yet—and we hope not ever! Even so, we cannot help but note how they are sometimes selfish, disobedient, disrespectful and deceitful. Oh yes, we forgive them and we love them still. But if we are honest we have to admit that there is something wrong with them.

Finally, and most reluctantly of all, we see a similar moral disorder in ourselves. In our quieter moments we cannot help but feel that we ourselves are guilty of considerable wrongdoing. Not rape, not murder, certainly! But so much else! We have not been as loving or as kind or as loyal or as honest or as diligent or as decent as we should have been. We know it, and it troubles us. We feel guilty. We feel ashamed. We feel disappointed with ourselves.

Strangers, loved ones, self—all confirm there is something radically wrong with human beings. But what?

As already noted, the Bible answers this question. It says that the problem with mankind is sin. At heart, all people are sinners—that is, they desire and do things that are wrong, things that deviate from God's moral standards, things that are hurtful to themselves and others. This moral corruption is so deep that,

16

although we can partially restrain it, we can never of our own accord entirely conquer it.

This is how the Bible expresses our problem: the human "heart is deceitful above all things" (Jer 17:9); "for out of the heart come evil thoughts, murder, adultery, sexual immorality, theft, false testimony, slander" (Matt 15:19); "there is no one righteous, not even one" (Rom 3:10); "all have sinned and fall short of the glory of God" (Rom 3:23).

Why does the Bible insist on presenting us with this dreadful picture of human nature—this dreadful picture of ourselves? One answer is that it is fundamentally concerned with the real and the true. It does not pretend things are other than they are. It does not pretty things up or play things down. It is realistic and truthful through and through.

The Bible's identification of us as sinners is not only realistic but also diagnostic. The Bible is making a diagnosis of our problem. What is the cause of this spiritual sickness that afflicts all people? It is sin, a corruption at the core of our being.

This is not a politically correct or personally comfortable diagnosis. But it is an honest and accurate one, and therefore an invaluable one.

It is a relief and a blessing to have a truthful diagnosis of our problem! What use is a doctor who tells us comforting things that are not true? The man with lung cancer might be relieved to be told that he has a common cold, but such a false diagnosis will kill him in the end. Oh, even if it is harsh, let us know the truth! If our problem is sin, by all means tell us. Then we can seek an appropriate treatment. How can we ever get healing without an accurate diagnosis?

The Bible does not speak of our sin because it wants to put us down, but because it wants to lift us up. God has truthfully diagnosed our problem because he wants to solve it. And he *has* solved it. He sent a Doctor to heal us. That Doctor is his one and only Son, Jesus Christ.

One of the names Christians have traditionally used for Jesus is "the Great Physician". This name is taken from a comment Jesus made to some self-righteous people who criticised him for associating with unworthy types. Jesus said: "It is not the healthy who need a doctor, but the sick. I have not come to call the righteous, but sinners to repentance" (Luke 5:31-32).

17

Gauging from this comment, Jesus plainly views us as sinners. Equally plainly, he views us with compassion. His heart is drawn to us. Seeing our misery, he laid aside his heavenly glory and came to earth as a doctor to heal us.

Before he could treat us, our Great Physician had to originate the treatment. Until he came, there was no adequate remedy for sin. So he pioneered one, the only one.

To heal us, Jesus needed to eradicate our sin—the guilt of it, the power of it, and the penalty due to it. To achieve this total eradication, he sacrificed his own life. "He himself bore our sins in his body on the tree, so that we might die to sins and live for righteousness; by his wounds you have been healed" (1 Pet 2:24). On the cross, Jesus set up an exchange. He took our spiritual sickness so that we could take his spiritual health.

By dying on our behalf and rising again from the grave, Jesus has brought about a perfect cure for our sin-sickness. That cure begins to take effect in our lives the moment we turn from our sin (repent) and trust in Jesus.

So, instead of being offended when God's word diagnoses us as sinners, we should humbly admit that it is right. Then we should call out to God's Son, the Great Physician, to make us well.

Only those who stand on their dignity and deny their own sin-sickness are beyond the Great Doctor's help. He will not force anyone to receive treatment. He will leave the self-righteous to argue their own case before God on the Day of Judgment.

As for those who admit that they are sin-sick and call out in faith to Jesus, they will indeed be made well. Their healing will begin immediately, and will be completed without fail in and for eternity.

Postscript: Words of diagnosis and healing from the Bible:

- Your iniquities have separated you from your God; your sins have hidden his face from you (Isa 59:2).
- The wages of sin is death, but the gift of God is eternal life in Christ Jesus our Lord (Rom 6:23).
- Christ died for sins once for all, the righteous for the unrighteous, to bring you to God (1 Pet 3:18).

- We all, like sheep, have gone astray, each of us has turned to his own way; and the LORD has laid on him the iniquity of us all (Isa 53:6).
- Look, the Lamb of God, who takes away the sin of the world (John 1:29).
- God so loved the world that he gave his one and only Son, that whoever believes in him shall not perish but have eternal life (John 3:16).
- Everyone who believes in him receives forgiveness of sins through his name (Acts 10:43).
- If you confess with your mouth, "Jesus is Lord," and believe in your heart that God raised him from the dead, you will be saved (Rom 10:9).
- These are written that you may believe that Jesus is the Christ, the Son of God, and that by believing you may have life in his name (John 20:31).

A Christmas Carol

While Christmas may not be a holy day for many people in our society, most people are happy to observe it as a holiday. And while few people know much about the meaning of Christmas, most still know some of the traditional songs of Christmas—songs known as "carols".

The music and lyrics of many Christmas carols are strikingly beautiful. Today they are probably the only Christian songs that are known (and even loved) by people in the wider community.

In one way or another, carols tell and celebrate the story of Christmas, which is the true story of the miraculous birth of God's Son, Jesus Christ, in Palestine over 2,000 years ago.

Some carols combine simple, narrative facts with insightful, theological truths—that is to say, they describe the account of Jesus' birth and relate the significance of it as well.

One such carol is "Hark, the Herald Angels Sing". Originally written by Charles Wesley over 270 years ago, this carol (now somewhat altered) has become a favourite among Christians and non-Christians alike.

The first line of the carol refers to the angels who heralded the birth of Jesus: *Hark! the herald angels sing.* These angels appeared one night to some shepherds who were caring for their flocks in the fields close to Bethlehem where Jesus was born. First the angel of the Lord spoke to these shepherds, then a multitude of angels sang to them (Luke 2).

The next three lines of the carol record the angels' message to the shepherds: *"Glory to the newborn King;/ Peace on earth, and mercy mild,/ God and sinners reconciled!"* These words are a poetic summary of what the angels said and sang. They declare that the newborn child is a King who has come to establish peace between holy God and sinful humans, a King whose reign will be marked by mercy towards those who welcome him as Saviour and Lord.

The final four lines of the first stanza record the song-writer's glad and urgent invitation to all people to join with the angels in praise and worship of Jesus: *Joyful, all ye nations, rise,/ Join the triumph of the skies;/ With the angelic host proclaim,/ "Christ is born in Bethlehem!"* Christianity is an inclusive religion, extending a genuine offer of salvation to all who will recognise Jesus as "Christ" (ie, God's chosen and anointed deliverer) and receive him as King.

The carol's second stanza begins with two lines that emphasise the majesty of Jesus: *Christ, by highest heaven adored;/ Christ, the everlasting Lord.* Jesus came to earth from heaven, where he enjoyed the adoration of the holy angels. And one reason why the angels adored him is because he was and is "the everlasting Lord". He is "everlasting", meaning that he had no beginning and has no end. He is "Lord", meaning that he has the same name, nature and authority as the Lord God Almighty, and so is worthy of the same love, reverence and adulation.

The majesty of Jesus portrayed in the first two lines stands in marked contrast to the humility of Jesus portrayed in the next two lines: *Late in time behold him come,/ Offspring of the Virgin's womb.* Jesus left heaven where he was adored by angels to come to earth where he would be despised and rejected by men. He came "late in time" in the sense that a long time elapsed between the first promise of his coming (Gen 3:15) and the fulfilment of that promise. He came as the *long-awaited* Messiah (or, Christ). And the way he came was through conception and birth.

However, the songwriter alerts us to something unique about Jesus' conception. He was the offspring not merely of a *woman's* womb, but of a *virgin's* womb. Jesus was not conceived through the natural process of sexual intercourse between a man and a woman. Rather, "the power of the Most High overshadowed" a virgin named Mary, and she conceived Jesus miraculously (Luke 1:35).

The next two lines of the second stanza celebrate the dual nature of Jesus: *Veiled in flesh the Godhead see;/ Hail the incarnate Deity.* Jesus is both fully man and fully God. Although his "Godhead" (his divine nature) was partly "veiled" (concealed) by his "flesh" (his human nature), it was not diminished. He was the incarnation, the embodiment, of God. Indeed, in him "all the fullness of the

21

Deity lives in bodily form" (Col 2:9). The newborn Jesus was no ordinary baby. The songwriter urges us to "see" and "hail" his deity in his humanity.

The final two lines of the second stanza emphasise Jesus' identification with us: *Pleased as man with men to dwell,/ Jesus, our Emmanuel.* Jesus became one of us so that he might live among us, sympathise fully with us and do everything necessary to save us. And he was "pleased" to do this! He did not come to earth grudgingly, or under compulsion. Despite the suffering that he knew awaited him, he came willingly and gladly.

The songwriter here mentions two names for the "newborn King", whom until now he has simply called "Christ". The first name is "Jesus", meaning "Saviour"—a name given to him shortly before his birth by an angel (Matt 1:21). The second is "Emmanuel", meaning "God is with us"—a name given to him seven hundred years before his birth by a prophet (Isa 7:14).

The first two lines of the third stanza present two more names for Jesus: *Hail the heaven-born Prince of Peace! Hail the Sun of Righteousness!* The title "Prince of Peace", first used by the prophet Isaiah (9:6), highlights the power of Jesus to establish peace in the lives of his people. The title "Sun of Righteousness", first used by the prophet Malachi (4:2), emphasises the majesty of Jesus as the one from whom the light of purity and truth shines forth.

The next two lines extend the image of Jesus as "the Sun of Righteousness": *Light and life to all he brings,/ Risen with healing in his wings.* Just as the sun is the source of all physical light and life, so Jesus is the source of all spiritual light and life. Further, as exposure to sunlight helps in the healing of physical wounds and mental depression, so exposure to Jesus heals the wounded soul.

The next line brings us back to earth, as it were: *Mild he lays his glory by.* Mildly, humbly, without fuss, this Prince of Peace, this Sun of Righteousness, laid aside his heavenly privilege and divine honour to become a baby.

The final three lines of the carol explain why Jesus came to earth as an infant: *Born that man no more may die,/ Born to raise the sons of earth,/ Born to give them second birth.* Jesus was born to be our Saviour. He came to deliver us from the death we deserve because of our wrongdoing. He came as a baby to the cradle so that he could go as a man to the cross to make amends to God for our sins. He was born so that we could have forgiveness and eternal life.

The salvation that Jesus won for us is likened to a "second birth" because it involves a whole new life-principle, a radical change in perspective and desire. Jesus himself said, "You must be born again" (John 3:7). This new birth, he said, requires the miraculous intervention of the Spirit of God. And God's Spirit intervenes to bring about this second birth whenever a person humbly believes in Jesus.

New life, abundant life and eternal life are promised to all who trust in Jesus—the Jesus who is both Man and God, the Jesus who is both Sacrifice and Saviour, the Jesus who is celebrated in the Christmas carol, "Hark, the Herald Angels Sing"!

An Easter Song

Because Christmas and Easter are central to Christianity, it is not surprising that Christians over the centuries have written numerous songs about them. Many of these songs commemorating the birth, death and resurrection of Jesus Christ are greatly loved by Christians and have been sung in churches for hundreds of years.

Some of the Christmas songs are known and loved even in the wider community. Indeed, attendances at Carols by Candlelight concerts in hundreds of parks around the nation during the Christmas season point to the ongoing popularity of these songs among people generally.

However, there is no corresponding appreciation in the community at large for the Easter songs of the Christian faith. They remain virtually unknown outside Christian circles. This is a pity because many of these songs are deeply moving and perceptive.

One fine Easter song, "A Green Hill Far Away", was written for children by an Irish woman, Cecil Frances Alexander, over 170 years ago, in the mid 1840s. Alexander wrote nearly 400 Christian songs and poems, including the famous Christmas carol, "Once in Royal David's City", and the familiar creation-celebration song, "All Things Bright and Beautiful".

"A Green Hill Far Away" is not one of Alexander's better-known works, but it deserves to be. In this Easter song, she draws our attention in a simple but insightful way to the setting, the mystery, the purpose, the necessity and the challenge of the crucifixion of Jesus Christ on the first Good Friday over 2,000 years ago.

The setting and scope of the crucifixion

The opening verse of Alexander's song portrays the setting and indicates the scope of the crucifixion.

> There is a green hill far away,
> Outside a city wall,
> Where the dear Lord was crucified,
> Who died to save us all.

The first two lines provide an emotional, as well as an actual, setting. They picture Golgotha (Calvary), the hill outside Jerusalem where Jesus was executed. But more than this, they allude to the loneliness Jesus experienced during his sufferings and are symbolic of his rejection by society. They echo the words of the Bible that Jesus "suffered outside the gate in order to sanctify the people through his own blood" (Heb 13:12).

The third line mentions the manner of Jesus' execution. He was crucified, nailed hand and foot to a wooden cross, lifted up and left to die. This was a particularly cruel and humiliating form of execution.

The last line of the first verse indicates the scope of Jesus' sacrifice: he "died to save us all". As the Bible says, Jesus went to the cross so that "he might taste death for everyone" (Heb 2:9); "he gave himself as a ransom for all" (1 Tim 2:6); "he died for all" (2 Cor 5:15). There is provision at the cross for everyone.

This is not to say that everyone will be saved. Only those who commit themselves to the Lord Jesus in repentance and faith will benefit eternally from his death. Nonetheless, by dying to save us all, Jesus demonstrated that we all need a Saviour and that we all may find a Saviour in him.

The magnitude and mystery of the crucifixion

The second verse of the song draws attention to the magnitude and mystery of Jesus' suffering.

> We may not know, we cannot tell,
> What pains He had to bear,

But we believe it was for us
He hung and suffered there.

The first two lines remind us that there is a depth to Jesus' suffering that is beyond our comprehension. We can only dimly imagine the physical torture he suffered during his trial and crucifixion. Yet the physical torment was only part of his suffering, and a lesser part, at that. The spiritual torment he endured was far more dreadful.

Because we are so comfortable with sin, Jesus' spiritual suffering is quite beyond our understanding. We cannot begin to imagine the revulsion he suffered when he was violated by our sins—when he who knew no sin was made sin for us (2 Cor 5:21). We cannot begin to imagine the agony he suffered when he endured God's wrath on our behalf. We cannot begin to imagine the depths of loneliness, horror and despair that caused him on the cross to cry out to his Father, "My God, my God, why have you forsaken me?" (Matt 27:46).

Although we do not know the depths of Jesus' agony, we do know the beneficiaries of it: "we believe it was for us/ He hung and suffered there". And, like Cecil Alexander, we can believe this because God's word teaches as a matter "of first importance" that "Christ died for our sins" (1 Cor 15:3). "[H]e was wounded for our transgressions … the LORD has laid on him the iniquity of us all" (Isa 53:5-6). Jesus died on our behalf and in our place.

The purpose of the crucifixion

"[W]hile we were still sinners, Christ died for us" (Rom 5:8). But why? What did he hope to achieve? Alexander explains the purpose of Jesus' death in the third verse of her song:

He died that we might be forgiven,
He died to make us good,
That we might go at last to heaven,
Saved by His precious blood.

Here we discover three reasons, three purposes, for the death of the Lord Jesus Christ.

Firstly, "He died that we might be forgiven"—forgiven by God for all that we have done wrong. The Bible states that "every one who believes in him [Jesus] receives forgiveness of sins through his name" (Acts 10:43). By his death, Jesus made amends for our sins, so that they need not be held against us anymore.

Secondly, "He died to make us good". We are not good in ourselves and we cannot make ourselves good. If left to our own merits and efforts, we could never avert God's judgment or obtain his approval. That is why God himself sent Jesus, his Son, to be our substitute. At Calvary our badness was transferred to him so that at conversion his goodness could be transferred to us. Our salvation begins with a borrowed goodness, but it does not end there. Having covered us with his goodness, the Lord Jesus then requires and assists us to become actually good. Hence, the Bible declares: "He himself bore our sins in his body on the tree, that we might die to sin and live to righteousness" (1 Pet 2:24).

Thirdly, Jesus died so "That we might go at last to heaven". Although hell is our desert, it need not be our destiny, thanks to Jesus and his sacrifice for us. He promises eternal life to all who believe: "Truly, truly, I say to you, whoever hears my word and believes him who sent me, has eternal life. He does not come into judgment, but has passed from death to life" (John 5:24).

The last line of the third verse—"Saved by His precious blood"—draws together the thoughts of the previous three lines. *Forgiveness, goodness, heaven*— all these amount to *salvation* and they have been made available to us by Jesus' death.

Alexander depicts his death, his blood, as "precious". And so it is: precious not only in its own right but also in its incalculable benefit to mankind. Jesus' sacrifice cost him his life and bought us eternal life. There can be no greater price and no greater purchase than that! The apostle Peter reminds Christians, "you were ransomed ... not with perishable things such as silver or gold, but with the precious blood of Christ" (1 Pet 1:18-19).

The necessity of the crucifixion

In the fourth verse of her song, Alexander explains the necessity of Jesus' death:

There was no other good enough
To pay the price of sin;
He only could unlock the gate
Of heaven, and let us in.

Jesus was the only one who could make amends for the wrongs we have desired, thought, said and done. Excluding Jesus himself, "all have sinned and fall short of the glory of God" (Rom 3:23). Jesus alone was "without sin" (Heb 4:15). He alone "knew no sin" (2 Cor 5:21). He alone "committed no sin" (1 Pet 2:22). This is why he, and he alone, could atone for our sins and become "the source of eternal salvation" for us (Heb 5:9).

"There was no other good enough" to do what had to be done to accomplish our salvation. This is one reason why Jesus himself said, "I am the way, and the truth, and the life. No one comes to the Father except through me" (John 14:6). By virtue of his unique and complete goodness and purity, Jesus is the only one who could "pay the price of sin" for us, and thereby "unlock the gate/ Of heaven, and let us in".

The challenge of the crucifixion

In the fifth and final verse, Cecil Frances Alexander explains the challenge of Jesus' death:

O dearly, dearly has He loved!
And we must love Him too,
And trust in His redeeming blood,
And try His works to do.

By his sacrificial death on the cross, Jesus showed us how dearly he loves us. And we ought to respond to his love in three ways: we ought to love him; we ought to trust him; and we ought to serve him.

This is the challenge that Easter presents to everyone. Bearing in mind that the Son of God loved us and gave himself for us (Gal 2:20), we should strive to love him in return, trust him without reserve, and serve him with resolution.

Inca Child Sacrifices

On a mountain top in the Andes 500 years ago three children were sacrificed to Inca gods. The two girls and one boy were drugged, buried alive, and left to die. Their mummified bodies were recently discovered by archaeologists and pictured in the press.

Although the archaeologists are not certain about the reason behind the ritual, it is likely that the Incas sacrificed the three children to appease their gods and to implore their blessing.

What should we make of such rituals today?

There is a tendency in the Western world to shy away from moral judgments about other cultures and religions. We are supposed to believe that one culture is as good as another and that all religions are equally worthy of respect. We are supposed to believe that good is relative and that evil is only in the eye of the beholder.

One of the archaeologists who discovered the dead Inca children seems to take this line. He claims that "They exude an air of tranquillity". He continues, "Their death was not violent, and this allows us to see the ritual from an Inca point of view: this was not a time of terror and horror but of peace and worship."[1] This is a clever try to put a good gloss on a bad happening, but it is not quite convincing.*

The photographs do not support the sentiment that the sacrificed children "exude an air of tranquillity." On the contrary, their faces exude all the usual vacancy and banality of death. Likewise, it requires a long stretch of the imagination to credit that the sacrifice "was not a time of terror and horror but of peace and worship." Who knows what torments of fear those three children suffered as they trekked the 22,000 feet to the mountain summit? Who knows what dread gripped them as the drugs took effect and they felt their minds slipping into blackness ahead of their bodies? Who knows how long they lived under the rubble and what horror they might have felt if they awoke from their stupor to discover they were buried alive and left alone to die?

And what drug, I wonder, was given to the three mothers to lessen the horror and grief they must have felt at the killing of their children? (Or are we to believe that those Inca mothers were an inferior sort, and lacked the maternal love so evident in mothers in our own society?)

We should not trivialise the deaths of those children by romanticising their culture or making excuses for their killers. There was a chilling brutality and barbarity at work on that mountain top 500 years ago. We do not have to consider ourselves morally superior to denounce those ritual killings as morally wrong. Certainly, from a Christian viewpoint, the sacrifice of those children was a monstrous evil.

The only thing we can say in defence of those ancient Incas is that they acted out of ignorance. And yet their ignorance was not total. There is a glimmer of truth in the midst of their darkness. They possessed (albeit in a weak and twisted way) two important insights.

The first insight involves a belief in the supernatural. The Incas rightly perceived that there is a spiritual dimension to the world. They rightly understood that there is something supernatural behind nature. They did not make the modern mistake of thinking that the universe consists only of matter. By believing in gods, they were closer to the truth than people today who believe in no God.

The Incas were right to believe in the existence of the supernatural, but they were seriously wrong in much of what they thought about it. They worshipped false gods, not the true and living God. This was their first, fundamental mistake. They believed in mountain gods and in the sun god. But no such gods exist. There is only one God. He is good and great. He is the Creator of all things, including the mountains, the sun and all mankind. He is the One who reveals himself and speaks to us in the sacred writings called The Bible.

The second glimmer of insight those ancient Incas had involves the matter of sacrifice. They perceived that the Deity demands a sacrifice. And in this they were quite right.

The Bible teaches that the true and living God is pure and holy. As a consequence, he is grieved and outraged by the wrong we all do, say, think and desire. Our sins separate us from him and bring us under his judgment. If we are to be reconciled to him and escape his wrath, he requires a sacrifice that makes amends for our wrongs. And that sacrifice must be a blood sacrifice, for the Bible declares that "without the shedding of blood there is no forgiveness" (Heb 9:22).

The Incas were right to think that God must be appeased by sacrifice, and a blood sacrifice at that. But this is where their understanding falters. For they were badly mistaken about what the sacrifice should be.

God does not want human sacrifice of any sort, and he expressly forbids child sacrifice. He commands: "Let no one be found among you who sacrifices his son or daughter ... Anyone who does these things is detestable to the LORD" (Deut 18:10-12). The Bible records that on one occasion the people of Israel broke this commandment and were condemned: "They shed innocent blood, the blood of their sons and daughters, whom they sacrificed to the idols of Canaan, and the land was desecrated by their blood. They defiled themselves by what they did ... Therefore the LORD was angry with his people" (Ps 106:38-40).

So, far from cleansing themselves by sacrificing those three children, the ancient Incas defiled themselves. Far from of appeasing God, they enraged him.

If it is not human sacrifice, is it animal sacrifice that God wants? Again, the answer is no. For although he commanded the people of Israel long ago to sacrifice animals, he never intended those sacrifices to remove sin. He intended them to be a reminder both of the seriousness of sin and of the punishment it deserves. But he expressly declares that "it is impossible for the blood of bulls and goats to take away sins" (Heb 10:4).

The prophet Micah expressed the fact that God does not want either animal or human sacrifice in these words (6:6-7): "With what shall I come before the LORD and bow down before the exalted God? Shall I come before him with burnt offerings, with calves a year old? Will the LORD be pleased with thousands of rams, with ten thousand rivers of oil? Shall I offer my firstborn for my transgression, the fruit of my body for the sin of my soul?" The answer is, No, no, no, no!

Where does this leave us, then? God requires a sacrifice to forgive our offences; that sacrifice must involve the shedding of blood; but it cannot be a human or an animal sacrifice. This surely places us in an impossible situation!

But thankfully, what is impossible for us is possible for God.

In spite of his just and holy anger towards us, God looked upon us in mercy and love. He saw our untenable position. He saw that we had no way to make amends to him for our sins. He saw that no animal is an adequate sacrifice because no animal has as much value as a human being. He saw that no human being is a worthy sacrifice because no human being is pure and sinless. And so he acted to provide the sacrifice himself.

God ordained that his eternal Son should enter the world and permanently assume our humanity in order to become our sacrifice. And his Son, whom we now know as Jesus Christ, willingly did this. He was not deceived or drugged or dragged. For love of his Father and for love of us, he chose to come to us, become one of us, and die for us.

Because of his dual nature and his pure character, Jesus was a perfect sacrifice. As a man, he was an equivalent sacrifice for any human being. As God, he was an adequate sacrifice for every human being. And as the Righteous One, he was an acceptable sacrifice for sinful human beings. So God was unreservedly pleased with and appeased by his death on our behalf.

Jesus was "the Lamb of God, who takes away the sin of the world" (John 1:29). He was the Lamb foreshadowed by all the lambs previously sacrificed in Israel. He was the Lamb that God himself provided as our sacrifice.

Here we discover another way in which the ancient Incas were badly mistaken. They misunderstood not only what the sacrifice should be, but also who should make it. Like most people before and after them, they thought that they themselves had to provide the sacrifice. But in fact it was God who had to do it. Only God could provide a sacrifice sufficient to cover our sins, satisfy his holiness and avert his anger.

Only God could—and he did. He offered his own Son as "the propitiation for our sins" (1 John 2:2). He did this 1,500 years before those Incas killed those children on that mountain. Oh, if they had but known!

---

* Nearly nine years after the discovery of the child sacrifices, a museum in Salta, Argentina, put the mummy of the oldest of the three children on display.

Newspaper coverage of the exhibition was embarrassingly starry-eyed, with the 15-year-old girl being described in archaic and romantic terms as an "Inca maiden". The *West Australian* fantasised that the executed girl had a "serene gaze etched on her face" ("Inca maiden makes a stunning return – 500 years after she was sacrificed", 8 September 2007), while the *New York Times* blithely claimed that in the victim's day "it was an honor to be chosen" for sacrifice ("In Argentina, a Museum Unveils a Long-Frozen Maiden", 11 September 2007).

Devotional & Theological Concerns

Believing the Bible:
The Issue of Inerrancy

Before we can believe *in* the Bible we need to believe certain things *about* the Bible. To begin with, we need to believe that it is true, utterly true. This belief is expressed in the doctrine of biblical inerrancy, which I wish to define and defend.

Defining inerrancy

Essentially, the word "inerrancy" means "freedom from error". Hence, when we say that a document is inerrant, we are saying that it is without error. There are no mistakes in it.

"Inerrancy" means much the same as "infallibility": the two terms are virtually interchangeable.

The doctrine of inerrancy asserts that the Bible is completely without error. It is totally truthful and entirely reliable. It is infallible, inerrant.

As originally given

There is, however, one important qualification. The doctrine of inerrancy maintains that the Bible is without error *as originally given*. This places an emphasis on what the authors actually wrote. The original documents (known as "autographs") were entirely accurate and true.

Some people feel that this qualification turns the doctrine into a mere abstraction, as the original documents no longer exist. Four things need to be said in answer to this.

Firstly, while the originals no longer exist, we know of a certainty that they once did exist. The existence of a copy proves the prior existence of the original; for we could not have copies without there being originals from which the copies were made. Given that there were once original documents, it is important for us to consider what their nature must have been.

Secondly, our attitude to the originals will affect our attitude to the copies. If we believe that the originals were marred by error, then we must inevitably believe that the copies are also marred, only more so.

Thirdly, our attitude to the originals will affect our attitude to textual scholarship. For if we believe that the originals were without error, then we will also believe that in reconstructing the originals we are reconstructing an inerrant Bible. Hence textual scholarship is of great importance to Christians who believe in inerrancy.

Fourthly, Christ and the apostles did not possess the original documents but this did not undermine their belief in the accuracy and reliability of Scripture.

The absence of the original documents does not invalidate the doctrine of inerrancy, nor does it turn the doctrine into a mere academic exercise.

Certainly, over the centuries the original documents have been lost and the copies that survive vary from one another in minor ways. These textual variations have to be evaluated in order to determine what the authors originally wrote. However, biblical scholars have been able to determine the wording of the original documents with great certainty. And in so far as we have recovered the original wording we possess the inerrant Word of God.

Approximately 97% of the Bible we have today accurately duplicates, word for word, what was originally written by the prophets and apostles. Dr Harold Lindsell states:

> Anyone who has doubts about the accuracy of the Scriptures that have come down to us by transmission through copyists is misinformed. We can say honestly that the Bible we have today is the Word of God. This is not to deny the existence of textual problems ... But the textual problems are minimal. Thus it is, that one of the world's foremost New Testament scholars, F.F. Bruce, has this to say in response to those who claim that infallibility is void because we do not have the original documents, and because of variant readings we cannot get

back to them: 'The variant readings about which any doubt remains ... affects no material question of historic fact or of Christian faith and practice.'[1]

Biblical inerrancy begins by affirming the reliability of Scripture as originally given and ends by affirming the reliability of Scripture as preserved in our age.

Inerrancy and inspiration

The doctrine of inerrancy is merely a logical extension of the doctrine of inspiration that Scripture teaches concerning itself. When we recognise that the Divine Author of Scripture is "the Spirit of truth" (John 14:7; 15:26; 16:13), we cannot escape the conclusion that everything he has inspired is truth-full. The Spirit of truth could not have inserted error into or conveyed error through Scripture, for it is impossible for him to lie or to be mistaken.

Some people point out that, while the Holy Spirit is infallible, his co-authors, the prophets and apostles, were fallible. Consequently, they say, the human authors could have—indeed, must have—made mistakes in what they wrote. This ignores the truth that the human authors spoke "as they were carried along by the Holy Spirit" (2 Pet 1:21; NIV). The Spirit was at work in the minds of the writers, guiding their thoughts and investigations not only to reveal truth to them but also to preserve them from error as they wrote. If God can work through a sinful woman to give us the sinless, incarnate Word, he can surely work through fallible men to give us the inerrant, written Word. Lindsell rightly observes, "It is no more strange that ... Scripture should be free from error than that the human Jesus born of the Virgin Mary should be free from original sin."[2]

The Spirit's work of preservation

Christians often acknowledge the work of the Holy Spirit in inspiring the Scriptures through the prophets and the apostles. However, we are apt to overlook that the Holy Spirit has been at work throughout the ages to preserve the Scriptures.

Paul notes in 1 Cor 2:6-16 that the Holy Spirit (1) searched out the deep things of God, (2) revealed them to the prophets and apostles, (3) motivated these men to write them down, and (4) guided them as they wrote.[3] It is

37

inconceivable that the Holy Spirit should go to such trouble and then abandon his work to the ravages of time and the vagaries of men.

The inspiring Spirit is also the preserving Spirit. This is why our Lord could say, "Heaven and earth will pass away, but my words will not pass away" (Matt 24:35; cf 5:18).

The word "inerrancy"

It has been argued that inerrancy is not an acceptable doctrine because the word "inerrant" does not appear in Scripture. However, the Church encapsulates a number of biblical doctrines in terms that do not appear in Scripture. The doctrine of the Trinity is a good example. Nowhere does the term appear in Scripture, yet it admirably conveys (in shorthand, as all terms do) the clear and comprehensive teaching in Scripture that God is one Being existing in three Persons.

Similarly, the doctrine of inerrancy succinctly and accurately conveys the inescapable conclusion that if the Word of God is inspired by the Spirit of God, it must be free from deliberate or inadvertent error.

While it does not actually use the word "inerrant", Scripture clearly affirms its own inerrancy. It asserts about itself that it is entirely truthful and trustworthy in whole and in part. Psalm 119, for example, celebrates the purity and perfection of God's Word. In verse 96, the psalmist declares: "I have seen a limit to all perfection, but thy commandment is exceedingly broad." In contrast to everything else, there is no end, no limit, to the perfection of God's Word.

Those who believe in inerrancy are not arguing for the word but for the concept. Like the psalmist, we believe that "the words of the Lord are flawless, like silver refined in a furnace of clay, purified seven times" (12:6, NIV). "Inerrancy" is, quite simply, a term that expresses this biblical concept. If a better term can be found to express the same concept, well and good.

Varying interpretations of inerrancy

Some people argue against the doctrine of inerrancy on the grounds that the term may mean different things to different people. However, different people have different understandings of the term "inspiration". Is this an argument against using that term? I think not. Nor is it a legitimate argument against the use of a term like "inerrancy". Rather, it is an argument for proper education of all Christians by pastors and theological lecturers. If the doctrine were being taught in our churches and colleges and study groups, people would not be confused about it.

Love versus inerrancy

Some people feel that discussions on the inerrancy of Scripture are divisive and therefore ought to be avoided. They point to the need for unity and brotherly love. Interestingly, people who argue this way often appeal to Scripture for support.

I once received a phone call from a Christian leader who told me that Christians ought to forget about inerrancy and give priority to loving one another. I responded, "How do you know that we ought to love one another?" The man became indignant. "From the Bible!" he said. "Precisely!" I replied. "Even our understanding of the nature and value of love is dependent upon the Bible. Yet by throwing a shadow on the Bible you throw a shadow even on the commandment to love one another, for how can I be sure that that commandment is not one of the errors in the Bible?"

The inculcation and preservation of a reverence for Scripture is not in conflict with the outworking of love. Quite the reverse. The preservation of a high view of Scripture ought to be seen as an act of love because it is a prerequisite of love. Our very understanding of the nature and function of love is dependent upon Scripture. More than this, for love to be genuine and enduring it must be built upon what is true.

The same applies to unity. Unity itself cannot be our highest goal because it is derived from the attainment of another goal—namely, an understanding of, and commitment to, what is true. When Jesus prayed for unity among Christians, he first asked the Father to "Sanctify them in the truth"; he then explained, "thy word is truth" (John 17:17). In this way, he emphasised the primacy not only of the truth but also of the Bible, which is the embodiment of truth.

Inerrancy and authority

How we view the inerrancy of Scripture will affect how we view the authority of Scripture. Logically, if the Bible is not free from error in whole and in part, it cannot be fully authoritative. For it must forfeit its authority at that point where it contains error. The man who believes that there are errors in the Bible cannot rationally submit himself wholly to its authority. For in doing so, he would inevitably, at some point, be submitting to error.

A belief in the inerrancy of Scripture provides a rational basis for a belief in the authority of Scripture, which in turn provides a rational basis for obedience to Scripture.

Concerning the relationship between inerrancy and authority, Dr J.I. Packer declares:

> When historic Christianity receives the Bible as an absolute authority for creed and conduct, it does so on the basis that since God is a God of truth and righteousness, that which he lays before us in writing must have the same qualities. The current inerrancy debate about whether we should treat all Bible teaching as true and right is really about how far we can regard Scripture as authoritative.[4]

The early Protestants were well aware of the essential interrelationship between inerrancy (ie, infallibility) and authority, as is evident from their creeds. The 1689 Baptist Confession of Faith (London), for example, speaks of "our full persuasion and assurance of the infallible truth, and divine authority" of Scripture, and declares that "The Holy Scripture is the only sufficient, certain and infallible rule of all saving Knowledge, Faith and Obedience".

The Bible is the believer's sole authority in matters of faith and conduct. It alone is fully authoritative because it alone can be relied upon to speak without error. *Sola scriptura*, Scripture alone: this is one of the great doctrines of the Reformation, which stands or falls on the inerrancy of the Bible.

History and creation

The doctrine of inerrancy asserts that the Bible is reliable not only in matters of faith and conduct but also in matters of history and creation. Indeed, as all these matters are interwoven, the accuracy of one affects the accuracy of another. As stated by Harold Lindsell, inerrancy means that the Bible

> communicates religious truth, not religious error. But there is more. Whatever it communicates is to be trusted and can be relied upon

as being true. The Bible is not a textbook on chemistry, astronomy, philosophy, or medicine. But when it speaks on matters having to do with these or any other subjects, the Bible does not lie to us. It does not contain error of any kind.[5]

Religion, history, science: the Bible does not err in its statements on any of these matters. Indeed, as all these matters are interwoven, the accuracy of one affects the accuracy of another. The doctrines of sin and salvation, for example, rest upon the literal truthfulness of the opening chapters of Genesis. The creation of Adam and his fall into sin are no less historical realities than the incarnation of Christ and his crucifixion. Indeed, the first events necessitated the second, which the apostle Paul recognises when he declares, "as one man's trespass led to condemnation for all men, so one man's act of righteousness leads to acquittal and life for all men" (Rom 5:18).

Dr Francis A. Schaeffer warns that some evangelical Christians do not mean what might be supposed when they claim to believe in the truthfulness and trustworthiness of the Bible. When pressed, it becomes apparent that they separate doctrine and conduct from history and creation, claiming that Scripture is reliable concerning the former but not the latter. For this reason, Schaeffer says, any doctrinal statement on Scripture must declare plainly that "the Bible is without error not only when it speaks of values, the meaning system, and religious things, but it is also without error when it speaks of history and the cosmos."[6]

Even if we classify creation and history as minor in comparison with faith and conduct, mistakes in those matters could have major ramifications. For it is hardly sensible to trust Scripture in the big things if it cannot be trusted in the small. If the God who was there cannot tell us how sin entered the world, why should we believe him when he tells us how sinners can enter the Otherworld? And if the Creator cannot accurately tell us how we came to have life, why should we believe him when he tells us how we should live?

Problems of an "errancy" view

As with other doctrines, an inerrancy position involves some difficulties. This needs to be acknowledged. But it would be a mistake to believe that the problems are all one-sided. The "errancy" position is also problematic.

Those who oppose the doctrine of inerrancy must consider questions such as these: How do you adhere to the full inspiration of Scripture if you believe that it contains errors? If there are errors in Scripture, how does this reflect on the character of the Spirit of Truth? If God was unable to work through sinful men to give us a perfect written Word, can we still believe that he was able to work through a sinful woman to give us a perfect incarnate Word? If God was unable to communicate with us perfectly, what does this say about his sovereignty? If the Bible is untrustworthy on "small" things, is it sensible to trust it on "big" things? If Scripture is errant, how can it be fully authoritative? If it is errant, who will determine which passages we are to believe and which we are to reject?

The problems surrounding an inerrancy view are less serious both in nature and in consequence than problems surrounding the contrary view.

Conclusion

A belief in the inerrancy of Scripture is both biblical and logical. Such a belief requires faith and humility, and encourages a reverential attitude towards the Word of God. Those who study the Scriptures with humility and reverence soon discover with David (Ps 19:7-10) that:

> The law of the Lord is perfect
> reviving the soul;
> the testimony of the Lord is sure,
> making wise the simple;
> the precepts of the Lord are right,
> rejoicing the heart;
> the commandment of the Lord is pure,
> enlightening the eyes …
> the ordinances of the Lord are true,
> and righteous altogether.

Perfect, sure, right, pure, true: these are the characteristics of Scripture that Scripture claims for itself; and these are the characteristics of Scripture that the doctrine of inerrancy affirms. This is why Christians should affirm the doctrine.

The Supreme Importance of the Unity of God

Unity is one of the attributes, one of the characteristics, of God.

While "unity", as a theological term, may be unfamiliar to some Christians, most Christians would be familiar with the divine attribute it describes. Both the word and the attribute are easily definable.

"Unity" means the same thing in theology as it does in mathematics: "one". The English word comes from the Latin word, *unitas/unus*, meaning "one". *The Concise Oxford Dictionary* defines "unity" as "oneness, being one or single or individual".

So when we speak of the unity of God, we are speaking of his oneness, his singleness, his solitariness. God is numerically one.* He stands alone. He is one of a kind. He is unique. There are no gods apart from him. The Bible plainly and repeatedly asserts this truth. For example:

- Hear, O Israel: The LORD our God is one LORD (Deut 6:4).
- See now that I, even I, am he, and there is no god beside me (Deut 32:39).
- For all the gods of the peoples are idols; but the LORD made the heavens (Ps 96:5).
- Before me no god was formed, nor shall there be any after me (Isa 43:10).
- I am the LORD, and there is no other; besides me there is no god (Isa 45:5).
- I am God, and there is no other; I am God, and there is no one like me (Isa 46:9).
- Jesus answered, "The first [commandment] is, 'Hear, O Israel: The Lord our God, the Lord is one'" (Mark 12:29).

- [W]e know that "no idol in the world really exists," and that "there is no God but one" (1 Cor 8:4).
- [F]or us there is one God (1 Cor 8:6).
- God is one (Gal 3:20).
- There is … one God and Father of us all, who is above all and through all and in all (Eph 4:4-6).

Each of these passages assert the unity, the uniqueness, the singularity, the oneness, of God. And many other passages in the Bible do the same. In fact, according to one theologian, "No other truth of the Scripture, particularly of the Old Testament, receives more prominence than that of the unity of God."[1]

In his self-revelation known as the Bible, God has laid great emphasis on his unity, his oneness. He repeatedly asserts that he is one of a kind, without predecessor or successor, without equal or rival. This being the case, we must conclude that the divine unity is an important matter, and we must further conclude that it has a significant bearing on our lives. But how and why?

There are at least six reasons why it is important to understand that there is only one God—the living God who created the heavens and the earth, the triune God who reveals himself in his written word, the Bible, and his incarnate Word, the Lord Jesus Christ.

A better knowledge of God

The first practical application of this truth is that it helps us to know God more accurately and fully. The Prophet Hosea urged, "let us press on to know the LORD" (6:3). Learning about God's unity is a necessary part of pressing on to know him.

Sometimes Christian people make an artificial division between the theological and the practical. But there is nothing more practical than getting a right understanding of who and what God is. Every truth about God is valuable precisely because it is a truth about God—our Creator, our Sustainer, our Redeemer, our Eternal Home. If we want to love God more, we need to learn more about him. It is wonderful simply to understand that the God we worship is unique in his being and nature and is the only God in existence. Knowing this truth encourages us to stand in awe of him and paves the way for us to love him more.

An answer to polytheism

A second practical benefit that flows from knowing about the unity of God is perhaps the most obvious one: It answers the error of polytheism, the worship of many gods.

Polytheism, as opposed to monotheism, was a major factor in the ancient world. Wherever Christians went they were confronted with the worship of numerous gods. The account in Acts 17 of Paul's visit to Athens illustrates this. When he entered Athens, Paul's "spirit was provoked within him as he saw that the city was full of idols" (v.16).

"That's all very well," some might think, "but it's history. Sure, an appreciation of God's oneness helped early Christians to counteract the error of polytheism, but we aren't confronted with that error in our society today." However, such thinking is mistaken. A few moments' reflection reveals that polytheism is very much alive and well in our society—and it is on the increase.

One of the fastest growing religions in the Western world is polytheistic. That religion is Mormonism, or the Church of Jesus Christ of Latter-day Saints. Mormons teach that "three separate gods rule our planet—the Father (Elohim), the Son (Jehovah), and the Holy Ghost." The foremost of these three is the Father, who himself was once "a man on another planet ruled by his heavenly Father. After faithfully obeying all the Gospel laws and ordinances, and being married to a wife (or wives) for eternity, he died, was resurrected, and was exalted to godhood. He now rules this, his own planet, on which we, his children, born of his wife, live. Every Mormon man who follows the same path can expect to become a god like Father Elohim, and organize and populate his own world. This process has been going on eternally, so there are billions of gods throughout the vastness of space."[2] That is what the Mormons believe. That is what they have in mind when they come to your door with the name of Jesus on their lips and the Bible in their hands, pretending to be merely another Christian denomination. They are polytheists who claim that God the Father is one god among billions, a god just like the one they themselves hope to become.

Mormonism is not the only polytheistic religion flourishing today in Western societies like Australia. Another is Hinduism, the religion of hundreds of millions of Indians. The main Hindu gods are Brahma, the creator, Vishnu, the preserver, and Shiva, the destroyer. But in addition to these three leading gods there are approximately thirty million lesser Hindu gods. And in case anyone thinks that this is of concern only to missionaries in India, remember that there is an increasing Indian population in Australia. Certainly, many Indian immigrants are not Hindus, but many are; and they are bringing the worship of their gods into our country.

The New Age Movement, which began in the 1970s and continues today under the guise of New Spirituality, is also polytheistic. While reading through a New Spirituality magazine[3] some time ago I noticed that it was full of claims about the divinity of human beings. One writer declares, "YOU are GOD", and states that your purpose on earth is "to evolve through all experience to become God realized again." Another writer, claiming to channel a message from the Archangel Michael, tells readers, "you are a . . . SPARK of GOD", and states that you need to visualise what you want "and then let your Divine Self create the miracle". Yet another writer urges readers to "trust in the GodSelf" and to "open up to the God within". These claims are typical of New Age or New Spirituality teaching. When asked how she felt about playing God in a forthcoming film, the singer Alanis Morissette replied that the role was not difficult because "Kevin Smith [the director] and I both believe that God is us."[4] The New Age/ New Spirituality is not something remote from us. Its adherents and its influences are all around us. And its primary emphasis is that human beings are gods, or may become gods, or may ally themselves with gods.

Whether through Mormonism or Hinduism or the New Age movement, polytheism is alive and well in Australia today. And ultimately the only answer to it is the unity of God. Christians must believe and assert as never before: *There is only one God! You are not a god! I am not a god! Spirits are not gods! The gods of other religions are not gods! The Father, Son and Holy Spirit—he alone is God!*

The same God for all

Here is a third way that this great truth is beneficial: The unity of God helps us understand that God is the God of all people. If there is only one God, then plainly no individual or nation can lay exclusive claim to him. Paul makes this point in Rom 3:29-30. He asks: "is God the God of Jews only? Is he not the God of Gentiles also?" Then he answers, "Yes, of Gentiles also, since God is one; and he will justify the circumcised on the ground of their faith and the uncircumcised through their faith." Paul's argument is this: Since there is only one God, he must be the same God for everyone; and since he is the same God for everyone, he must relate to everyone in the same way. If he cares for these people he also cares for those people; if he requires faith of these people he also requires faith of those people. There's no distinction. If there were many gods, then perhaps *our* God is not for *them*. But as there is only one God, then inevitably *our* God is *their* God, too.

Because it is monotheistic, Christianity is by nature a generous, universal religion. The God who made us is the same God who made our neighbours. The God who gave his Son for us is the same God who gave his Son for our neighbours. The God who justified us when we believed is the same God who will justify our neighbours if and when they believe. Once we realise that *God is one*, we begin to realise that he is the God for *everyone*. Thus the unity of God becomes a basis for evangelism and offers hope to all people. It is because of the unity of God that we can say to others: "Our God is your God, too. And what he has done for us he can do for you."

The same Saviour for all

The fourth application is closely related to the last one: The unity of God reveals that there is only one Saviour for all people.

The Lord says in Isaiah 45:22, "Turn to me and be saved, all the ends of the earth! For I am God, and there is no other." The unity of God is the rationale for the exhortation to all people to turn to God. If there is only one God, then there can be only one Saviour. "Turn to me ... *for* there is no other to turn to!"

Turning to Allah, the God of Islam, is futile because Allah does not exist. Trusting in Brahma or Vishnu is pointless because all the Hindu gods are delusions. Calling to the goddesses of Wicca is useless because such goddesses are mere wishful thinking. The only God who can save us is the God of the Bible because he is the only God there is.

When we Christians say that salvation cannot be found in other faiths, we are not being arrogant, but realistic. We are simply stating a fact. Of all the world's religions, only Christianity offers salvation because only Christianity recognises and reveres the one, true triune God.

Because of the unity of God, the Christian faith is an *exclusive* faith. And yet for the very same reason, the Christian faith is also an *inclusive* faith. Isaiah 45:22 brings out both aspects: "Turn to me and be saved, all the ends of the earth! For I am God, and there is no other." While it is true that only the Christian God can save, it is also true that this same God invites "all the ends of the earth" to trust in him and be saved.

So then, Christianity is *exclusive* in that it claims that it alone offers a way of salvation, but it is *inclusive* in that it invites all people to follow that way. And the basis for both the exclusion and the inclusion is the unity, the oneness, of God.

The same moral standard for all

A fifth practical benefit that flows from the doctrine of God's unity concerns mankind's morality.

The oneness of God clarifies that there is only one moral standard—one standard of goodness—for all people. If there is only one God who by his nature, example and command sets the standard for all that is good, then that standard of goodness does not and cannot alter from culture to culture or nation to nation or individual to individual. What is good for one is good for all: what is evil for one is evil for all.

If there were many gods, there could be many standards of right and wrong. What one god forbids, another might command. What disgusts one god might delight another. In Deuteronomy 12:31, the true God, the God of Israel, condemns practices involved in the worship of false gods, the gods of Canaan. He warns the Israelites not to imitate the Canaanites, declaring, "every abominable thing which the LORD hates they have done for their gods; for they even burn their sons and their daughters in the fire to their gods."

Now, suppose for a moment—if we can do so reverently for the purpose of clarification—suppose that the God of Israel is only one of many gods, and that the gods of Canaan are also true and living gods. If that were so, surely the Canaanite gods would have as much right to command certain practices from the people of Canaan as the Israelite God has to command certain practices from the people of Israel. If the Canaanite gods deemed it good for the people of Canaan to sacrifice their children by fire, then who is the God of Israel to object to this practice? He is just one of many gods, after all.

But the truth is that the LORD is *not* just one of many gods. He is the *only* God. There are no gods beside him. Therefore, there are no standards of goodness beside him. He alone establishes what is right and wrong, good and evil.

Divine unity determines human morality: One God, one good! One sovereign over all, therefore one standard for all!

This is why Christians have the moral authority to oppose certain cultural and personal practices. If particular customs do not meet the one true standard of goodness commanded and exhibited by the one true God, then Christians can and should oppose them. So, for example, in times past Christians rightly opposed the practice of cannibalism in Papua New Guinea. They rightly opposed the practice of forcing young girls into temple prostitution in India. They rightly opposed the practice of wife-sharing and the sexual path-making ceremonies of the Australian Aborigines. And in contemporary times, Christians rightly oppose the practice of female genital mutilation and honour killings in Muslim communities locally and overseas. They rightly oppose the practice of pre-marital and extra-marital and same-gender sex in Australia and other Western nations. They rightly oppose the practice of sacrificing unborn children to the gods of hedonism and materialism through abortion in the Western world.

Christians have not opposed such practices because they consider themselves superior to other people, nor because they have some arbitrary objections to them. Rather, they have been compelled to act by the fact that there is only one God, and therefore only one standard of goodness and holiness for everyone.

Undivided devotion to God

A sixth practical application is this: The unity of God teaches us that there must be a unity in our love for God. Our affections must not be divided, for God alone is worthy of our full devotion, and he is one. This is the teaching of Deuteronomy 6:4-5: "Hear, O Israel: The LORD our God is one LORD; and you shall love the LORD your God with all your heart, and with all your soul, and with all your might." The command to love the Lord earnestly with our whole being is based on the fact that the Lord is one.

The logic goes like this: if there are no other gods, then there are no other legitimate claimants on our devotion and worship. The LORD our God is one LORD. And because he alone is God, he alone is deserving of our adoration and allegiance. "Who is like you, O LORD, among the gods? Who is like you, majestic in holiness, terrible in glorious deeds, doing wonders?" (Exod 15:11). Who is like you? Not one! You are unique, unmatched in splendour, power, justice, goodness and grace—therefore we will love you with all our heart, soul and might. There are no other gods to divide our devotion.

Conclusion

Moses declared to Israel in Deuteronomy 4:35: "To you it was shown, that you might know that the LORD is God; there is no other besides him." The same can be said of the church: *To us it has been shown, that we might know that the LORD is God; there is no other besides him.* What should we do with this knowledge, this revelation? To begin with, we should oppose the many gods that are being held up in our society and exalt in their place the one true God. We should strive to introduce all people to God, knowing that our God is our neighbour's God, too. We should share the good news that the one and only Saviour provided by the one and only God invites all peoples and every person to come to him and be saved. We should practice and proclaim clear biblical standards of righteousness, knowing that there is one good for all because there is one God of all. And we should determine to love God with all that we are and all that we have, knowing that there is no one else worthy of our undivided devotion.

Devotion to God necessarily involves devotion to the gospel of his dear Son, Jesus Christ, who by his death on the cross made amends for the sins that separate us from God. So it is fitting to conclude this study with a comment on the connection between the unity of God and the gospel of Christ.

Salvation depends on an understanding of the unity—the oneness—of God. When speaking to God the Father in prayer on one occasion, Jesus said, "this is eternal life, that they know you the only true God, and Jesus Christ whom you have sent" (John 17:3). As is evident from the first part of this statement, coming to a realisation that there is only one true God is essential for salvation.

However, believing in the unity of God is not enough. It is necessary, but it is insufficient. The Apostle James warns, "You believe that God is one; you do well. Even the demons believe—and shudder" (2:19). The demons know that there is only one God, but they do not benefit from the knowledge. It does them no good.

To benefit eternally from the knowledge of God's oneness we need to be introduced to God. And the good news is that God himself has sent a mediator, a go-between, to make such an introduction possible. The Apostle Paul states in 1 Timothy 2:5, "there is one God, and there is one mediator between God and men, the man Christ Jesus". To meet God in peace and friendship, we must first meet Jesus in repentance and faith. When we turn from our sins and trust in him, he introduces us to God the Father, who welcomes us with the gifts of adoption and eternal life.

---

* While the Bible teaches that there is only one God, it also teaches that the Father is God, the Son is God and the Spirit is God. Recognising that Scripture cannot contradict itself, Christians rightly reconcile these truths in the glorious doctrine of the Trinity, which teaches that three distinct Persons share without distinction a single divine essence. Hence, the unity of God is compound in nature: it is a tri-unity, being three-in-one.

The Question of Truth

In response to Jesus' claim that his "kingship is not of this world", Pilate asked, "So you are a king?" Jesus answered, "You say that I am a king. For this I was born, and for this I have come into the world, to bear witness to the truth. Every one who is of the truth hears my voice." Pilate responded, "What is truth?" (John 18:37-38).

"What is truth?" This has become a famous question, not only because of the context in which it was asked, but also because of its abiding relevance to the human condition. Pilate may have asked the question with sarcasm or cynicism, but it is nonetheless a serious question that every person must ask and answer.

"What is truth?" This is not an abstract question for many young people today. It is a question that is being thrust upon them by their teachers and their text books. Students studying literature in upper high school and at university, for example, are being confronted with theories and philosophies that effectively deny the existence of truth. Structuralism, Marxism, postmodernism, humanism, New Ageism—our young people are being encouraged to adopt these worldviews and to apply them in their analysis of literature and in their practice of life. Yet, one way or another, all these ideologies insist that truth is relative and subjective.

Postmodernists, for example, claim that "all truth is relative to one's peers or community" and, consequently, "there is no eternal truth or truth that is true around the world."[1] New Agers claim that "truth resides within each individual and, therefore, no one can claim a corner on the truth or dictate truth to another."[2] Either position leads to the view that there is no universal right or wrong answer to any moral, aesthetic or theological question: there is only each individual's conviction of what is right and true. And of course, your opinion is true for you, as mine is for me; and I can accept your "truth" as true *for you*, despite the fact that it contradicts what I believe is true *for me*.

Christianity rejects such notions of truth. It rejects the idea that truth is arbitrary and transitory. It rejects the idea that truth is entirely a human concoction, varying from one age to another, from one society to another, from one group to another, and from one individual to another. It rejects the idea that a thing is true as long as it serves socialist or feminist or humanist utopian goals. It rejects the idea that a thing is true if I (or you) feel it is true and can persuade other people to feel similarly. It rejects the idea that what is true for me can be quite different from what is true for you.

According to the Christian worldview, truth is real, not illusory. Truth is God-given, not manmade. Truth is eternal, not temporal. Truth is absolute, not arbitrary. Truth is objective, not subjective. Truth is universal, not regional. Truth must be respected, not manipulated.

So, for example, the fact of God's existence is not conditional upon our belief or disbelief, but represents the same unalterable reality for me as it does for you. The text "Jesus died for our sins" is not dependent on our agreement or interpretation, but rather communicates the same basic meaning to me as it does to you. The command "You shall not commit adultery" is not dependent on our acceptance or obedience, but rather places the same moral obligation on me as it does on you. The reality of God's existence, the meaning of God's word, the obligation of God's standards—these represent objective and absolute truth, truths that are unaltered by local culture and unaffected by personal preference.

Jesus distilled the Christian understanding of truth when he told Pilate that he had come "to bear witness to the truth". This statement reveals three basic facts about truth. Firstly, truth is real. There *is* such a thing as truth. Jesus could hardly bear witness to the truth if it were a myth or an illusion. The fact that he came to bear witness to it is proof that it exists. Secondly, truth is important. It has weight and worth. Indeed, it is so significant that its promotion justifies great sacrifice. If this were not so, Jesus would not have left heaven to bear witness to it. Thirdly, truth is knowable. Jesus *could not* bear witness to the truth if he himself did not know it; and he *would not* bear witness to it if he did not believe that he could communicate it. His bearing witness to the truth demonstrates that he knows it and that he believes he can help us to know it, too.

"For this I was born, and for this I have come into the world, to bear witness to the truth," Jesus said. And in saying it, he revealed that truth is real and important and knowable. More than this, he also revealed what truth is.

Indeed, Jesus actually answered the truth question before Pilate asked it. For if he came "to bear witness to the truth" then the truth must be what he bore witness to. So, to answer the question, "What is truth?", we must pose the question, "To what does Jesus bear witness?" And the answer to this question lies on every page of the Bible. The enduring teachings of the Bible—teachings about the existence of God and of good, teachings about God's image-bearers and our fall from grace, teachings about God's standards and his requirements of us, teachings about God's Son and his mission to save us—these teachings are the truths to which Jesus bore witness. And they are recorded in the Bible with such accuracy and clarity that Jesus was able to say to the Father, "Thy word is truth" (John 17:17).

The Lord Jesus is deeply concerned with the truth. He told the Samaritan woman, "God is a spirit, and those who worship him must worship in spirit and truth" (John 4:24). He told his fellow Jews, "If you continue in my word, you are truly my disciples, and you will know the truth, and the truth will make you free" (John 8:31-32). He also said to them, "[I have] told you the truth which I heard from God" (John 8:40). He called the Holy Spirit, "the Spirit of truth" (John 14:17; 15:26); and he promised his disciples that "When the Spirit of truth comes, he will guide you into all the truth" (John 16:13).

The Gospel of John closely identifies Jesus with truth. John indicates that Jesus is both a storehouse and a supply channel for truth: he is "full of grace and truth" and "grace and truth came through" him (1:14, 17). Jesus himself indicates that he is at one with the truth: he said, "I am the way, and the truth, and the life" (14:6). These statements show that Jesus and truth are not only interrelated but also intermingled. They are intimately united, fused together and dissolved into each other like two metals in an alloy. Indeed, truth can no more be separated from Jesus than light can be separated from the sun. He is full of truth; the truth comes through him; he is the truth.

Now this casts the truth in a new light. "What is truth?" Pilate asked. But in a sense he got the question wrong. It is not *what* but *who* is truth? Truth is not abstract, it is Personal. For Jesus is himself the truth from whom all truth flows and on whom all truth depends and through whom all truth can be known. Without Jesus we can never gain an understanding of the truth. We can only steal fruit from the tree of the knowledge of good and evil. It is only when we become Jesus' disciples that we know the truth, and the truth sets us free.

The Way of the Samurai

Books have a way of haunting us. One that has haunted me over the years is a collection of anecdotes and reflections by Yamamoto Tsunetomo, a samurai retainer of the Nabeshima Clan in 17th and 18th century Japan. Yamamoto's utterances were arranged as a book titled *Hagakure* ("In the Shadow of Leaves")[1] just three years before his death in 1719.

Hagakure is a study of *Bushido*, the Way of the Samurai. The samurai were the warriors of ancient Japan, expert with bow and sword, fierce in battle, obsessed with honour, and self-sacrificing in the cause of their lords.

Throughout the book, Yamamoto often uses the term "retainer" for "samurai" because a samurai was by definition a man "retained" in the service of someone of rank. Indeed, the word "samurai" means literally "those who serve". A masterless samurai, a *ronin*, was an oddity, and was generally viewed either with pity (his master having died) or with misgiving (his master having dismissed him from service).

Hagakure offers a fascinating insight into the mindset of the ancient samurai and the customs of ancient Japan. It has been described as "the most influential of all samurai treatises ever written". Yamamoto's thoughts not only reflected but also shaped the ideals of Japan's warrior class over many centuries. They help to explain the bravery, abandon and brutality of the Japanese fighting men even into the middle of the twentieth century.

The thing that impressed me most while reading *Hagakure* was the samurai ideal of loyalty and service to his lord. Although I could not agree with Yamamoto's every expression of this ideal, I did find myself wholeheartedly endorsing the concept of it. Indeed, Yamamoto's treatise set me thinking about my Lord and the quality of my devotion to him.

According to Yamamoto Tsunetomo, this is the Way of the Samurai in relation to his lord:

- "Every morning one should first do reverence to his master … For a warrior there is nothing other than thinking of his master."
- "Not to forget one's master is the most fundamental thing for a retainer."
- "Being a retainer is nothing other than being a supporter of one's lord, entrusting matters of good and evil to him, and renouncing self-interest."
- "Whatever you do should be done for the sake of your master … Doing something for one's own sake is shallow and mean and turns to evil."
- "A retainer is a man who remains consistently undistracted twenty-four hours a day, whether he is in the presence of his master or in public. If one is careless during his rest period, the public will see him as being only careless."
- "Loyalty is … important in the pledge between lord and retainer."
- "[I]f a warrior makes loyalty and filial piety one load, and courage and compassion another, and carries these twenty-four hours a day until his shoulders wear out, he will be a samurai."
- "[W]hen it comes to the point of throwing away one's life for his lord, all get weak in the knees. This is rather disgraceful. The fact that a useless person often becomes a matchless warrior at such times is because he has already given up his life and has become one with his lord."
- "Concerning martial valour, merit lies more in dying for one's master than in striking down the enemy. This case can be understood from the devotion of Sato Tsugunobu [who was mortally wounded while intercepting arrows fired at his lord]."
- "Even when the children in his family were very young, Yamamoto Jin'emon would draw near to them and say, 'Grow up to be a great stalwart, and be of good use to your master.' He said, 'It is good to breathe these things into their ears even when they are too young to understand.'"
- "A person who serves when treated kindly by the master is not a retainer. But one who serves when the master is being heartless and unreasonable is a retainer."
- "To try [by fawning or forwardness] to enter the good graces of the master is unbecoming. One should consider first stepping back and getting some

understanding of the depths and shallows and then working without doing anything the master dislikes."

- "A man is a good retainer to the extent that he earnestly places importance in his master."
- "But even a person who is good for nothing and exceedingly clumsy will be a reliable retainer if only he has the determination to think earnestly of his master."
- "If one were to say in a word what the condition of being a samurai is, its basis lies first in seriously devoting one's body and soul to his master."

Yamamoto presents an astonishing picture of the thinking of the ancient samurai in relation to their lords. With our emphasis today on individuality and independence, such thinking is utterly alien to us. Yet it is precisely the sort of thinking the Bible encourages in relation to Jesus Christ.

The central declaration of the Bible, which is the definitive treatise about Jesus, is simply and profoundly this: "Jesus is Lord!" (1 Cor 12:3). Jesus is the Lord of heaven and earth: "he is Lord of lords and King of kings" (Rev 17:14). And because "he is Lord of all" (Act 10:36), he is the rightful Lord of every person in the world, demanding and deserving our entire loyalty.

An acknowledgement of, and submission to, Christ's Lordship is the starting point of the Christian life: "if you confess with your lips that Jesus is Lord and believe in your heart that God raised him from the dead, you will be saved" (Rom 10:9).

Those who make this confession must continue in it. Once we acknowledge Jesus as Lord, we must accommodate him as Lord: "Therefore, as you received Christ Jesus the Lord, so walk in him" (Col 2:6). And it seems to me that this is where the example of the samurai is so helpful.

As Yamamoto thought about *his* Lord, so we Christians should think about *our* Lord. We should name and revere him when we wake in the morning, think about him all day long, endeavour to understand the depths of his mind and will, defer to his judgment in all matters of good and evil, support him in his cause, be prepared to lay down our lives for him, do everything for his sake rather than our own, devote body and soul to him, and seek to become one with him. In short, we should be fully and continually loyal and responsive to him.

And surely Jesus is worthy of such devotion. If the samurai were prepared to devote themselves to lords who were only human, how much more should we be prepared to devote ourselves to a Lord who is both human and divine? If the samurai were prepared to give loyalty to lords who could be "heartless and unreasonable", how much more should we give loyalty to a Lord who is always reasonable and kind?

Too often we Christians live like *ronin*, masterless samurai. We roam where we please. We confess with our lips that Jesus is Lord, but not with our lives. It is time we followed the Way of the Samurai in the service of our Lord.

Yamamoto speaks to Christians across centuries and cultures. He shows us the meaning of lordship. He challenges us to place ourselves entirely at the disposal of *our* Lord. And he assures us that, with dedication, even the least of us may become "a reliable retainer" and "a matchless warrior".

Yamamoto helps us to see that, like the Way of the Samurai, the Way of the Christian is a way of loyalty. Only, our loyalty is to the Lord of lords—and as such it is immensely more necessary and noble!

Engraved on God's Hands

The Lord asks his people in Isaiah 49:15, "Can a woman forget her sucking child, that she should have no compassion on the son of her womb?" How would we, his people today, answer that question, I wonder?

If the question were put to mothers with infants, I expect they would answer with a resounding, "No!" Women simply do not forget the infants who grow in their wombs and suckle at their breasts. On the contrary, such is the strength of their love that mothers can hardly put their children out of their minds, even when it is necessary and good to do so. "No," we want to answer, "a woman cannot forget her sucking child!"

But this is not the answer that God gives. He says, "Even these may forget ..." What a shocking thought! As unlikely and as unnatural as it seems, God says, even mothers, of all people, can forget their infants and lose their love for them.

God is not saying this in order to cast aspersions on a mother's love. Rather, he is saying it to emphasise his own love. A mother's love is powerful—so powerful that it is almost unbreakable—but God's love is greater. There is no "almost", no "perhaps", no "what if", in God's love. It is given with the full backing of, and has the same character as, his absolute holiness and his infinite power. Even nursing mothers may forget their infants, yet, the Lord declares, "yet I will not forget you."

Well, if a mother's love is not adequate to express the power and permanence of God's love, what is? The Lord offers this picture: "Behold," he says, "I have graven you on the palms of my hands ..." (Isa 49:16). That is to say, "I have cut your name into my palms in the same way that an engraver cuts a word into a stone. I have carved you onto myself—that is how permanent my love is for you!"

Of course, the Lord is speaking figuratively. He is trying to help us understand his love by drawing a picture of it. Yet there is a sense in which we may take it literally. For 2,000 years ago, as foretold in Isaiah 7:14, a virgin conceived and bore a son, whose name was Immanuel, meaning "God is with us". This foetus, this infant, this boy, this adolescent, this man, Jesus, was God incarnate, God come in human flesh. Indeed, as the apostle Paul declares, "in him all the fullness of God was pleased to dwell"; and again, "in him the whole fullness of deity dwells bodily" (Col 1:19; 2:9).

It pleased God, who is Spirit (John 4:24), to assume a physical body in the man Jesus. Jesus had a physical body just like ours. He had—and still has—limbs and organs just like us. And it is upon the hands of Jesus that God has engraved a reminder of us.

At Calvary, the hands of the Son of God were nailed to the cross for us. He was wounded for our transgressions (Isa 53:5). And to the present day, even as he sits this very moment at the right hand of God making intercession for us (Heb 8:1; 7:25), his hands bear the marks of his sacrificial love. The moment the nails were hammered home at Calvary, we were forever written upon his hands.

We Christians can sometimes doubt that Jesus still loves us. We can sometimes doubt that, having saved us, he will keep us to the end. At such times, we need to hear his post-resurrection words to Thomas: "Put your finger here, and see my hands ... do not be faithless, but believing" (John 20:27). When we see and touch by faith the hands that were pierced for us, we appreciate anew that Christ's love for us is as permanent as the scars he got to save us.

The cross provides assurance for all Christians, for it reminds us of the strength of our Saviour's love. It reminds us that, although we sometimes forget him, he never forgets us. Indeed, he has promised, "I will not forget you. Behold, I have graven you on the palms of my hands".

When Christians Take Their Lives

Some time ago I conducted a funeral for a man who committed suicide. This man, Glen, was my friend. And he was a Christian.

Since the funeral, various people have asked for a copy of the message that I gave at the graveside. And it has occurred to me—and to Glen's widow—that others might benefit from it, too.

So, to people suffering from suicidal thoughts, and to people suffering from the loss of a loved one by suicide, and to pastors who must present the truth with love in the face of such suffering—I offer this message of caution and comfort.

Dear people, we are gathered here today in tragic circumstances. And the only thing I can think to do is to deal with that tragedy head-on. The fact of Glen's death is sorrow enough, but the manner of his death adds sorrow to sorrow.

As most of you would know, Glen was troubled by depression for various reasons for much of his life. In recent months his depression became quite severe, and although he sought the help of doctors and friends, he could not break free of it. Then last week he tried to break free by taking his own life.

What Glen did was wrong. Indeed, the sense of bewilderment and hurt that infects our grief today is testament to just how wrong it was. We must leave our deaths in the hands of the Lord who gave us our lives. Suicide is wrong. That needs to be said. But there are many other things that need to be said, too.

It needs to be said that sometimes a person—*and a Christian person at that*—can fall into such a dark place that he can see no light at all. How and why he fell is not the issue here. The issue is that a person *can* fall. Darkness veils Christ's lovely face to such a degree that he loses all sense of Christ's unchanging grace. And so he does a desperate thing.

It also needs to be said that suicide is *not* the deciding factor in a person's salvation. A Christian who takes his own life will have something to answer for on that account, but he will not be cast out on that account. We are not saved by grace through faith … *plus obedience.* We are saved by grace through faith … *plus nothing!* "Whoever calls on the name of the Lord will be saved" (Acts 2:21, Romans 10:13). And once a person has called and been saved, what can separate him from his Saviour? Can "tribulation, or *distress,* or persecution, or famine, or nakedness, or peril, or sword?" No, no, never! "For I am sure that neither death, nor life, nor angels, nor principalities, nor things present, nor things to come, nor powers, nor height, nor depth, *nor anything else* in all creation, will be able to separate us from the love of God in Christ Jesus our Lord" (Rom 8:35, 38, 39). Dear people, we are saved not by our faithfulness to Jesus, but by his faithfulness to us.

It also needs to be said that a man is not saved by the *strength* of his faith, but by the *fact* of his faith. Glen, it seems, had many questions and many difficulties concerning the Christian life. But he did not doubt the truth of the gospel, the good news that Christ died for our sins and rose again from the dead, so that whoever believes in him will be saved. Glen believed the gospel, and he called on the name of the Lord and was saved. You know, the stronger a man's faith in God, the stronger his experience of God's love: the weaker his faith, the weaker his experience. But irrespective of the strength or weakness of his faith and experience, the *reality* of God's love for him is unaltered. Even if Glen's faith was as small as a mustard seed, it was sufficient in Christ to move a mountain of sin from between him and his God.

And finally, it needs to be said that Jesus is very tender towards his people, and never more so than when they are suffering. Jesus knows that sometimes people—*his people*—can get so low that they can see no way out. He knows that sometimes people can feel such despair that they are moved to desperation. And he does not look on his people in these circumstances with anger and severity and condemnation, but with sympathy and kindness and yearning.

The Gospel of Matthew records how John the Baptist fell into despair after King Herod put him into prison. John felt so low that he began to doubt that Jesus really was the Lamb of God come to take away the sin of the world. He felt so low that he even sent his disciples to ask Jesus, "Are You the Expected One, or shall we look for someone else?" (Matt 11:3, NASB) This man who had spent his life making a straight path for Jesus now said to Jesus, "Are you the One? Are you really the Son of God and the Saviour of the world? Are you? Are you?" And the Bible tells us that after Jesus confirmed by miracles that he truly was the Expected One, he turned to the people around him and talked to them about John. And this is what he said: "Truly I say to you, among those born of women there has not arisen anyone greater than John the Baptist!" (11:11). Oh, don't you see it? Just when John thought the worst thing he had ever thought about Jesus, Jesus said the best thing he had ever said about John.[1] Jesus was not angry with John. He did not rail against John because of his doubt and his despair. On the contrary, he loved John all the more!

Jesus will not, he simply will not, "break a bruised reed or quench a smouldering wick" (Matt 12:20). He is very tender towards his people. And he is very tender towards Glen, as Glen now knows.

Dear people, I tell you these things in the name and for the glory of the Lord Jesus Christ, that man of sorrows who was deeply acquainted with grief. Put your trust in him. Take your comfort from him. For

> Jesus knows all about our struggles,
> He will guide till the day is done
> There's not a friend like the lowly Jesus
> No not one, no not one.[2]

Making Sense of Disaster

Disasters strike mankind with great frequency and variety. Most of the "smaller" ones go unreported, and are known only to the friends and relatives of the victims. The "larger" ones, however, usually make the news headlines, and arouse feelings of bewilderment and loss in the wider community.

Earthquakes, floods, fires, shootings, crashes—how do we make sense of such disasters? In particular, how do we make sense of why they happen to whom they happen? Why did *that particular disaster* happen to *those particular people*? Why did it happen to *them* (or, to *us*)? This is a question that has troubled mankind for thousands of years.

The Jewish people in the time of Jesus, for example, were troubled by it. On one occasion news spread abroad of two disasters. One involved people from Galilee who were slaughtered by the Roman governor, Pilate. The other involved people in Siloam who died when a tower collapsed on them.

When questioned about these disasters, Jesus said (Luke 13:1-5, NIV):

Do you think that these Galileans [whose blood Pilate mixed with their sacrifices] were worse sinners than all the other Galileans because they suffered this way? I tell you, no! But unless you repent, you too will all perish. Or those eighteen who died when the tower in Siloam fell on them—do you think they were more guilty than all the others living in Jerusalem? I tell you, no! But unless you repent, you too will all perish.

Jesus' statement must have shaken his countrymen. They generally believed that people got what they deserved. So to their way of thinking, a person who died in a shocking way must have been a particularly bad person.

But Jesus utterly rejected this notion. He insisted that the people who had died in the disasters were no worse than the people standing before him. Or to put it another way, the people standing before him were no better than those who had died.

In saying this, Jesus ruled out the conjecture that all disasters are God's judgment on especially bad people. God (by his wrath) is not always the active cause of disasters, nor are victims (by their wickedness) always the passive cause.

It is true that God can directly intervene in nature and in human affairs to achieve his purposes. And the Bible records many instances of such divine interventions. It is also true that sometimes those interventions are expressions of God's judgment. But Jesus indicates that, unless there is some compelling reason to do otherwise, disasters should not be interpreted as "acts of God", and disaster victims should not be regarded (and should not regard themselves) as especially bad people whom God has singled out for punishment.

Jesus rules out one possible answer as to the cause of disasters generally. This is very helpful. It preserves us from dark superstition about God, callous speculation about those who have suffered, and smug satisfaction about ourselves.

Interestingly, Jesus does not go on to say what the cause of disasters *is*. He contents himself with saying what the cause is *not*. We might be wise to content ourselves with that, too.

And yet perhaps Jesus' words offer a clue as to why disasters happen. Perhaps his disclosure of the negative clears the way for our discovery of the positive. For if God does not always directly and deliberately produce disasters to punish bad people, then it is reasonable to conclude that sometimes disasters must happen because of the way the world is. And two basic things can be said about the way the world is. Firstly, it is a causal world—that is, it is a world in which cause and effect are at work. Secondly, it is a ruined world—that is, it is a world in which both nature and human nature are in disarray.

The reason our world is a causal world is because God has made it that way. He made it so that this-leads-to-that according to fixed laws of nature and morality.

The reason our world is a ruined world is because it has been corrupted by Man and cursed by God. Human beings corrupted the world because they chose

66

to rebel against God and his goodness, thereby causing massive disruption to the natural and moral order. God cursed the world and subjected it to futility in response to mankind's sin (*cf* Gen 3:16-19; Rom 8:20), thereby bringing all people under a general and ongoing judgment.

So then, the (natural and human) world inevitably behaves as God intended as far as cause and effect is concerned. And this ordained principle of causation can be catastrophic when operating in a ruined world—a world on which God has placed a curse and in which he permits moral corruption.

Ironically, it appears that the cause of disasters is often the exact opposite to the one imagined by the crowd to whom Jesus spoke. Far from occurring because God *does* intervene in natural and human affairs, many disasters occur because God *does not* intervene. They occur because he permits things to proceed along the lines that he ordained when he originally created the world as a place in which all things interconnect and interact according to natural and moral laws. They occur because he allows one thing to lead to another. This means that, in a ruined creation, storms *will* arise and wreak havoc—they simply *will!* It means that, in a ruined heart, malice and greed *will* arise and wreak havoc—they simply *will!*

Disasters occur when God permits the world he cursed and we corrupted to function in a causal way. They occur when God stands back. But thankfully he often steps in. Without doubt there would be many more disasters were it not for his active intervention. So far as his intervention in the natural world is concerned, we cannot say much. Who knows what storms, what earthquakes, what floods would have occurred had he not stopped them? When it comes to human affairs, however, we can cite millions of instances of his gracious intervention. For every Christian person is a living proof that God acts in the world to divert disaster. How many more murders, how many more cruelties, how many more deceptions would there be in the world were it not for God's cleansing intervention by his Son and his Spirit in millions of sinful human hearts?

If he chooses, God *can* bring disasters upon individuals or nations as punishment. But, according to Jesus, he generally chooses not to do this. Rather, he generally allows things to proceed according to the natural and moral principle of cause and effect. This means that in a world that is now in disarray because of human sin, nobody is immune from disaster.

In our efforts to make sense of disaster, we should not automatically suppose that the victims are somehow personally at fault. Certainly, to the degree that disasters are part of God's general judgment (curse) on our sinful world, and to the degree that we are all sinners deserving punishment, every disaster victim has justly tasted something of the wrath of God. But that, in a sense, is beside the point. Jesus' point is that we should not suppose that God has singled out victims of disaster for special punishment. The specific cause of the particular disaster is not to be found in them. They are people just like us—no better, no worse.

But while Jesus rules out the idea that disaster victims are especially bad wrongdoers, he reminds us that all people are guilty of wrongdoing. And while he rules out the idea that disaster victims are especially subject to divine judgment, he reminds us that all people will be judged. "Unless you repent," he warns, "you too will perish."

Whether or not they have a moral origin, disasters certainly have a moral function. They remind us of our mortality and our accountability. They remind us that we are all going to die, and then we are all going to give an account of how we lived. They bring us to our senses. And this, from Jesus' perspective, is the heart of the matter. The important thing is not that we make sense of disasters, but that we make sense of ourselves in the light of them.

"Man is destined to die once, and after that to face judgment" (Heb 9:27). One way or another, death will come to us all. And when it does, so will God's full and final judgment. This will be the ultimate disaster—unless we repent.

Choose the Right Counsellor

There has been a proliferation of counsellors in our society in recent times, with a corresponding proliferation of people going for counselling. Depending on their concerns, troubled souls can seek help from marriage counsellors, grief counsellors, trauma counsellors, depression counsellors, self-esteem counsellors, anger-management counsellors, life-goals counsellors—and more besides.

Christians, too, have become keen on counsellors and counselling, with some denominations and churches offering both counselling services and counselling courses. Yet, ironically, at a time of unprecedented interest in counselling, Christians seem to have largely forgotten the greatest counsellor in human history: Jesus Christ our Lord.

Scripture says of Jesus, "For to us a child is born, to us a son is given; and the government shall be upon his shoulder, and his name shall be called Wonderful Counsellor ..." (Isa 9:6). Jesus is *the* Wonderful Counsellor, and his people should call upon him as such.

A counsellor is someone who gives advice and guidance. Jesus willingly counsels all who call on him, and his counsel is always wonderful. And the reason that he is such a wonderful counsellor is because he has in abundance all the qualities that a person needs for counselling.

There are four qualities that combine to make a good counsellor. I deduce this not from studying textbooks on counselling and psychology, but from thinking the matter through from a biblical perspective. On reflection, a good counsellor requires sympathy, virtue, knowledge and wisdom.

These qualities are our Lord's qualifications. He is a wonderful counsellor because he possesses these wonderful characteristics to a wonderful degree. He is deeply sympathetic, perfectly virtuous, fully knowledgeable and infinitely wise.

Characteristics: Sympathy

Sympathy is the first characteristic of a good counsellor. People in need of counsel are also usually in need of kindness and warmth. A gruff, uncaring person will not make a good counsellor.

Jesus is a sympathetic man. Indeed, his sympathy for us is apparent from both his identification with us and his compassion on us.

The extent of his identification with us is evident from Isaiah's statement that "to *us* a child is born, to *us* a son is given". In order to associate and share with us fully, Jesus came to us, and became one of us. The Son of God came to earth as a human being, adopting our nature and sharing our circumstances. Consequently, he knows all about suffering and temptation, and so he is able to sympathise with us in our weaknesses (Heb 2:18 & 4:15). The incarnation is the measure of Jesus' identification with us.

Jesus' sympathy is seen in the care and compassion he has for us. Isaiah prophesied of him: "He will feed his flock like a shepherd, he will gather the lambs in his arms, he will carry them in his bosom, and gently lead those that are with young" (40:11). Again, Isaiah declared, "a bruised reed he will not break, and a dimly burning wick he will not quench" (42:3). Speaking prophetically on Jesus' behalf, Isaiah said, "The Spirit of the Lord GOD is upon me, because the LORD has anointed me to bring good tidings to the afflicted; he has sent me to bind up the broken-hearted, to proclaim liberty to the captives, and the opening of the prison to those who are bound" (61:1).

The Son whom God has given to us is tender-hearted and compassionate towards us. The prophets foresaw this, and his life confirmed it. Remember how he "had compassion on" the widow of Nain and raised her dead son (Luke 7:13). Recall how he was "moved with pity" to heal the leper in Galilee (Mark 1:41). Bring to mind how "he had compassion for" the crowds wherever he went, "because they were harassed and helpless, like sheep without a shepherd" (Matt 9:36). And above all remember his sacrifice at Calvary. For it was love that led him to the cross to bear our grief, our sin, our guilt, and our punishment. He poured out his soul to death to save us. If the incarnation is the measure of Jesus' identification with us, then the crucifixion is the measure of his compassion for us. Little wonder scripture exhorts and explains, "Cast all your anxieties on him, for he cares about you" (1 Pet 5:7).

The Lord Jesus Christ is a wonderful counsellor because he fully sympathises with all who approach him for counsel.

And yet, sympathy is not enough. A sympathetic person does not necessarily make a good counsellor.

Think, for example, of a teenage boy and teenage girl who disregard Jesus' wonderful counsel that sexual intimacy is meant only for marriage. They sleep together and she becomes pregnant. In her distress she goes to a Family Planning centre for help. A counsellor listens to her troubles with obvious compassion, and even gives her a comforting hug. Then the counsellor advises the young woman that the best thing to do is to have an abortion. "Don't worry, you won't have to face this alone," the counsellor says kindly. "I'll book you in for the procedure myself, and on the day I'll come along for support." Now, there can be little doubt that this counsellor is a *sympathetic* counsellor, but she is hardly a *wonderful* counsellor. Indeed, for all its sympathy, her counsel is not wonderful, but diabolical!

So, sympathy is not enough. To be of value, it must be balanced with virtue.

Characteristics: Virtue

Virtue is the second characteristic of a good counsellor. People in need of counsel are also in need of moral integrity. A corrupt person will not make a good counsellor.

Again, Jesus meets the highest standard. He is not only a sympathetic man: He is also a virtuous man.

From the manger to the cross, Jesus was perfect and upright, and all that he did was righteous and just. Isaiah acknowledges Jesus' moral perfection when he states that Jesus will establish and uphold his eternal kingdom "with justice and with righteousness" (9:7).

Throughout his earthly life, the Lord Jesus went about doing and being good (Acts 10:38). He was the supreme model of moral excellence, a literal paragon of virtue. He committed no sin and merited no guilt (1 Pet 2:22). He lived a blameless life, without spot or blemish (Heb 9:14). Although "in every respect" he was "tempted as we are", he nonetheless remained "without sin" (Heb 4:15). And it is his moral purity that gives integrity to his counsel and makes it wonderful.

The integrity of a person's character will affect the integrity of his (or her) counsel. The counsel he gives will reflect the life he lives.

I recall dealing as a pastor with a Christian man who had set his heart to marry a non-Christian woman. He was determined to do it, even though he knew that God's word warns against a Christian marrying a non-Christian. This man also wanted to be a school chaplain—a role that would involve giving counsel to many young people, including ones from our church. And he needed my approval to take up that chaplaincy. But I refused to give it. I called the church elders together and we held a meeting with him. And one of the questions we put to him was this: "If a teenage Christian girl comes to you and asks for guidance about whether or not to marry her non-Christian boyfriend, what advice would you give her?" He replied that, provided they truly loved each other, he would advise her to go ahead.

When a man deliberately does something wrong, he feels a pressure to counsel others to do likewise. This may be because he genuinely believes that his own behaviour is right. Or it may be because he would feel himself a hypocrite to be doing one thing and yet counselling another. Or again, it may be because he longs to justify himself—and getting others to keep him company in the same sin is a way to quieten his own conscience and to strengthen his own resolve.

The moral tenor of a person's character and conduct will affect the moral tenor of his or her counsel. While this may be a disturbing truth in connection with certain counsellors today, it is a wonderful truth in connection with Jesus. For he has no sin to hide, no wrong to justify, no conflict to reconcile, no selfishness to serve—and so he has no motive to give false counsel. Indeed, it would never enter his heart to misuse or mislead those who confide in him. Because he is morally perfect and pure, all his counsel is morally perfect and pure, too. It is wonderful.

By virtue of his virtue, the Lord Jesus is a wonderful counsellor!

And yet virtue is not enough. A person may be virtuous, and even sympathetic, and yet lack adequate knowledge to be a good counsellor.

Characteristics: Knowledge

Knowledge, then, is the third characteristic of a good counsellor. An ignorant person can hardly give good advice.

To be effective, a counsellor must have some general knowledge about both human nature and God's purposes; and he must also have some specific knowledge about both the character and the predicament of the person whom he is counselling. It is impossible to give sound counsel without a measure of knowledge.

And Jesus, being God as well as Man, has knowledge beyond measure. He knows, quite literally, everything about everything. He certainly knows the ins and outs of human nature and of the divine will. And just as wonderfully, he knows everything about you and me.

Do you recall Jesus' encounter with Nathanael? As Nathanael approached him for the first time, Jesus said, "Behold, an Israelite indeed, in whom is no guile!" When Nathanael asked in surprise, "How do you know me?", Jesus replied, "[W]hen you were [sitting] under the fig tree, I saw you" (John 1:43-51).

Before we ever knew Jesus, he knew us. And he knows us now. He knows each of us individually through and through. He knows our past and our future. He knows our needs and our wants. He knows our joys and our hurts. He knows our thoughts and our acts. He knows our guilt and our innocence.

When Jesus met the Samaritan woman at the well, he laid bare the dark secrets of her life. And she hastened back to Samaria and said to the people, "Come, see a man who told me all that I ever did" (John 4:29). As with the Samaritan woman, so with us—Jesus knows all that we ever did, whether good or bad. And this comprehensive knowledge enables him to give wonderful counsel.

And yet, even knowledge is not enough to make a good counsellor. A person may have immense knowledge and yet lack the ability to assess and apply that knowledge in an intelligent and insightful way. This is where wisdom is necessary.

Characteristics: Wisdom

Wisdom is the fourth characteristic of a good counsellor. A person who lacks discernment and understanding will not make a good counsellor.

Thankfully, Jesus is wonderfully wise, as indicated by his name and his office. He would not deserve the title of "Wonderful Counsellor" if he were not exceedingly wise. Nor could he shoulder the government of his people without exceptional wisdom.

Isaiah says of Jesus, "the Spirit of the Lord shall rest upon him, the spirit of wisdom and understanding, the spirit of counsel and might, the spirit of knowledge and the fear of the Lord" (11:2). Wisdom, understanding, counsel and knowledge rest with Jesus—and they rest with him infallibly and to an infinite degree. He understands all reality and comprehends every insight, for he is the one "in whom are hidden all the treasures of wisdom and knowledge" (Col 2:3).

Jesus' wisdom is evident from the reaction of those who encountered him. As a child he "grew and became strong, filled with wisdom" (Luke 2:40). As a twelve-year-old boy he sat and conversed with the religious leaders in the temple "and all who heard him were amazed at his understanding" (Luke 2:47). Throughout his childhood and adolescence, "Jesus increased in wisdom and in stature and in favour with God and man" (Luke 2:52). In the early days of his ministry, the people of his hometown "were astonished" as he taught them in the synagogue, and they puzzled, "Where did this man get this wisdom?" (Matt 13:54), and they were offended that this wisdom was his own, and had not been imparted to him by doctors of theology and professors of psychology at reputable academic institutions. And it goes on.

When Jesus taught in the synagogue at Nazareth, all the people "wondered at the gracious words which proceeded out of his mouth" (Luke 4:22). When he skilfully answered the religious leaders concerning the payment of taxes to Caesar, "they marvelled" (Matt 22:22). When he taught in the temple, "The Jews marvelled at it, saying, 'How is it that this man has learning, when he has never studied?'" (John 7:15). And when the officers whom the Pharisees sent to arrest Jesus returned empty-handed, they explained their failure to carry out their orders by saying, "No man ever spoke like this man!" (John 7:46).

Furthermore, the wisdom of Jesus is apparent from the effect of his life and teaching on his disciples. When Peter and John defended the gospel before the Sanhedrin shortly after the Day of Pentecost, the religious leaders were impressed by their bold and persuasive arguments; and perceiving them to be uneducated, common men, "they wondered; and they recognised that [Peter and John] had been with Jesus" (Acts 4:13). That was the explanation for their wisdom—they had been with Jesus!

And to this day, being with Jesus makes a person wise. For example, bring even a child to Jesus and soon he will have more wisdom than a university professor. For that child will quickly learn the answers to the fundamental questions of life.

Where do we come from? God made us!
Why are we here? To love and serve God and each other!
Where are we going? To be with Jesus—or to be apart from him—forever!

A child who keeps company with Jesus knows the answer to these and other deep questions, while a university professor who keeps company with everyone but Jesus has no answers at all.

Jesus makes people wise. It is an astonishing thing. And there is no explanation for it except to acknowledge that Jesus himself is exceedingly wise and gives wonderful counsel to those who walk with him.

So then, the Lord Jesus Christ is a wonderful counsellor because he deals wisely with, and gives wisdom to, all who approach him for counsel.

In summary: Jesus is deeply sympathetic, perfectly virtuous, fully knowledgeable and infinitely wise, and this combination of qualities enables him to be a wonderful counsellor.

But how, exactly, can we access his counsel? How can we approach him? How can we hear him? After all, he is not physically present with us as he was with the original twelve disciples. So how does he counsel us now? What is the means of his counsel to us today?

There are four main ways that our Wonderful Counsellor gives his counsel, his guidance.

Means: The Scriptures

The Bible is the first means by which Jesus guides us.

The psalmist declares, "I have more insight than all my teachers, for I meditate on your statutes" (Ps 119:99). The scriptures counsel the receptive reader on every matter of creed, conscience and conduct; and their counsel gives him delight and insight, and safeguards him from foolish decisions and sinful actions. As King David says, "The law of the LORD is perfect, reviving the soul. The statutes of the LORD are trustworthy, making wise the simple" (Ps 19:7).

According to Psalm 119, it is through his written word that the Wonderful Counsellor offers: guidance in times of indecision and uncertainty—"Your word is a lamp to my feet and a light to my path" (105); renewal in times of discouragement and despair—"My soul clings to the dust; give me life according to your word!" (25); support in times of anguish and grief—"My soul melts away for sorrow; strengthen me according to your word!" (28); assurance in times of threat and persecution—"Even though princes sit plotting against me, your servant will meditate on your statutes" (23); and fortitude in times of illness and hardship—"If your law had not been my delight, I would have perished in my affliction" (92).

The Bible is the primary means by which Jesus counsels us. Those who want his wonderful counsel must meditate on his written word and be advised by it. They must be able to say with the psalmist, "Your testimonies are my delight, they are my counsellors" (24).

Means: The Spirit

The Holy Spirit is the second means by which Jesus counsels us.

We are not alone as we walk this life. Jesus did not leave us as orphans when he returned to heaven. He gave us a perfect replacement for himself—the Holy Spirit, "the Spirit of Christ" (Rom 8:9; 1 Pet 1:11).

Just before his crucifixion, Jesus identified the Spirit as a "Counsellor", a counsellor exactly like himself, and he comforted his disciples with the promise that "the Father ... will give you another Counsellor, to be with you for ever, even the Spirit of truth" (John 14:16-17). He explained that "the Counsellor, the Holy Spirit ... will teach you all things, and bring to your remembrance all that I have said to you" (John 14:26). And again, he said, "When the Spirit of truth comes, he will guide you into all the truth" (John 16:13).

Given that the Holy Spirit is the senior, superintending author of the Bible, it is hardly surprising that he uses the Bible as his chief means of counsel. Indeed, a crucial task of the Holy Spirit is to help us understand the scriptures. The Spirit who inspired the prophets and apostles to write also illuminates what they wrote. He enlightens us to the meanings of the scriptures. If we call upon him and lean upon him, the Holy Spirit will make the Book he authored in history a living letter in our lives today, a letter of intimate insight and comforting counsel.

While his written Word is the primary means by which the Holy Spirit speaks to us, it is not the only means. He can speak to us through our conscience and through our fellow believers (to which I will return shortly). He can speak to us through our circumstances, governing them in such a way that we are guided towards certain understandings and convictions. He may also sometimes "move" us emotionally and mentally, giving us a "sense" of what course to take or an "impression" of what to say and do. And he is always eager to hear us and to intercede for us—revealing our mind to God and God's mind to us (cf Rom 8:26-27 & 1 Cor 2:6-16).

Means: Our Conscience

Our Conscience is the third way Jesus guides us.

Paul declares, "I always take pains to have a clear conscience toward God and toward men" (Acts 24:16). Elsewhere, he states that "By rejecting conscience, certain persons have made shipwreck of their faith" (1 Tim 1:19). These two statements by the apostle alert us to the fact that we should take care to listen to our conscience and to follow it.

Our conscience is the moral faculty that God has given us to help us determine good from evil and to help us choose good over evil. Indeed, it is God's witness within us to the moral law that God has written in our hearts; and if we would "by nature do what the law requires," we must obey it (Rom 2:14-15).

The Bible never encourages us to disregard our conscience. Quite the reverse. We are always to heed it. But we are also to educate it. Because we are fallen our conscience is fallen also, and it can sometimes be in error. It can excuse us when it ought to condemn us, and condemn us when it ought to excuse us. Consequently, we need to educate it from God's word. Nonetheless, we are always to be mindful of it and to obey it. It is the moral light God gives to enlighten every person and it is a means by which our Wonderful Counsellor counsels us.

Means: Other Christians

Christian pastors and teachers are the fourth source of Jesus' counsel.

Paul states that one of the gifts Jesus gives to the church is pastors and teachers, through whom every member of the congregation is to be built up and brought to maturity (Eph 4:11). So, the Wonderful Counsellor gives wonderful counsel through pastors and teachers.

Some churches have learnt to their great sorrow that pastors can go horribly wrong and do great harm. But most pastors are Christlike. And the Lord Jesus uses the preaching and teaching of these godly pastors to give good counsel to his people.

Indeed, a pastor counsels his whole congregation on Jesus' behalf every time he preaches. This is one reason why biblical preaching is so important. It is a collective counselling that helps individuals firstly to avoid and secondly to overcome heartache and trouble.

It is no coincidence, then, that the growth in so-called Christian counselling services has paralleled the decline in Christian preaching. As Christians have grown less inclined to listen to faithful, biblical preaching, so they have become more inclined to seek personal counselling.

While pastors rightly counsel people in many private and individual ways, public preaching is the first and foremost way by which they counsel believers on Jesus' behalf. It is through preaching that the Wonderful Counsellor convinces, rebukes and exhorts his people. This being the case, it follows that pastors should make every effort to heed God's command to "preach the word" urgently, diligently and constantly (2 Tim 4:2). It also follows that Christian people should make every effort to attend church regularly in order to listen attentively to the preaching of God's word, and thereby receive Jesus' wonderful counsel through their pastors.

But, of course, it is not just pastors and gifted teachers through whom the Lord Jesus speaks. He gives counsel to his people through his people—*all* his people, *provided only* that they are living in harmony with him. Any mature Christian person who loves the Lord Jesus and knows his word is a person who is able, in some measure, to give wise counsel to others.

We should beware of the modern notion that the best (if not the only) people to counsel us are people who have degrees in psychology or diplomas in counselling. (And we should be especially wary of professional counsellors who claim to be Christians but who put secular theories above scriptural truths.) The best counsellors are those who are the best Christians. It is people who receive counsel *from* Jesus who are best suited to give counsel *for* Jesus. He will give us wonderful counsel through them.

Having said this, I hasten to add that there *is* a place for professional counsellors, including secular ones. Academically trained psychologists, psychiatrists, doctors, therapists and counsellors may be precisely what is needed in certain circumstances. Someone who is severely depressed, for example, may well need medical help, and he or she should take the anti-depressant medications that a psychiatrist or a doctor prescribes. The same could apply to someone who is suicidal. Someone who is struggling with alcoholism would do well to seek the assistance of a counsellor, a sponsor and a support group at Alcoholics Anonymous. And so on.

Furthermore, if it is true that Jesus can give good counsel through *all* his faithful people, then inevitably it is also true that he can give good counsel through professional counsellors who are faithful to him. Professional counsellors who are practising Christians can sometimes be a means by which Jesus advises and helps his people in their distress.

My argument is not primarily *against* the professional counsellor: it is principally *for* the Wonderful Counsellor.

Conclusion

We Christians have ongoing, open access to a counsellor who is deeply sympathetic, perfectly virtuous, infinitely knowledgeable, and profoundly wise. He is the Son whom God has given to us and his name is Wonderful Counsellor. But are we availing ourselves of his counsel?

In a world awash with counsellors, we should at least remember that Jesus is a counsellor, too. Indeed, he is the *chief* counsellor, and his counsel is always wonderful. Consequently, he should be the *first* one we turn to in times of trouble or sorrow or temptation or uncertainty. Those who make him their *first* counsellor generally find that he becomes their *last* counsellor. They need no other. For there is no other who understands us so intimately, loves us so dearly, and guides us so truly.

Marriage According to Scripture

From a Christian standpoint, marriage is crucial to the honour and happiness of the genders and the generations. It is the rightful home of sexual love and family life. It is a good gift from God.

To appreciate the gift as God intended, we need to turn to that great marriage instruction manual, the Bible. There we discover basic truths about: the origin of marriage; the nature of marriage; the purpose of marriage; government in marriage; sex in marriage; and children in marriage.

The origin of marriage

The opening chapters of Genesis reveal that marriage originates from God. He is its author on two counts—by creation and by command.

In the beginning, "God created man in his own image, in the image of God he created him; male and female he created them" (Gen 1:27). Marriage is possible because God made human beings male and female. Had he made us asexual like the angels there would be no marriage. But as it is, he made humanity as a duality—masculine and feminine. Consequently, men and women possess contrasting but complementary bodies and natures, thereby making it possible for one to fulfil the other in marriage.

Furthermore, God made human beings in his own image. Among other things, this means that we possess personality, conscience, intellect, and will. All these spiritual qualities are necessary for the relationship we call marriage. A ram and a ewe, a dog and a bitch, cannot marry because they lack the spiritual dimension that marriage requires. A man and a woman, on the other hand, may marry precisely because their natures are more than biology and instinct. As spiritual beings, we are capable of love and commitment. In short, because he created us in his image, God created us with the ability to enter into a *relationship* with each other.

God further established the foundations of marriage by the special creation of woman from man. After the Lord had made Eve from Adam's rib, he brought her to Adam, who said, "This at last is bone of my bones and flesh of my flesh; she shall be called Woman, because she was taken out of Man" (Gen 2:21-23). Men and women are related by image and by blood. Therefore we yearn for one another.

Having made marriage possible by his creative power, God then made it necessary by his moral decree. He proclaimed that because woman was taken out of man to be his companion, "a man leaves his father and his mother and cleaves to his wife, and they become one flesh" (Gen 2:24). God mandated marriage at the commencement of human existence. Marriage is morally imperative for any couple who wish to proceed in their relationship beyond a certain level of intimacy.

The nature of marriage

The essential characteristics of marriage can be discerned from a statement by the Lord Jesus Christ recorded in Matthew 19:4-6, where he cites and comments on Genesis 2:24. Answering a question put to him by the Pharisees about divorce, Jesus said, "Have you not read that he who made them from the beginning made them male and female, and said, 'For this reason a man shall leave his father and mother and be joined to his wife, and the two shall become one flesh'? So they are no longer two but one flesh. What therefore God has joined together, let not man put asunder." Six truths concerning the nature of marriage emerge from this statement.

Firstly, marriage is heterosexual. It is for male and female—not male and male or female and female. While this is a truism, such is the moral tenor of our age that some people are confused about it. But there is no confusion in Scripture. It condemns homosexual behaviour as biologically aberrant and morally abhorrent. The advocacy of homosexual marriage is nothing less than an attempt to clothe perversion in the robes of decency. *Have you not read that he who made them from the beginning made them male and female?* Marriage involves the union of members of the opposite sex.

Secondly, marriage is sexual. The first thing a man and a woman do when they are alone after their wedding is "become one flesh". Marriage involves intimate physical and spiritual union between a man and a woman.

Thirdly, marriage is monogamous. It permits *one* man to unite with *one* woman for life. Christ clarifies this by the way he cites Genesis 2:24. While the use of the singular for "man" and "wife" in Genesis 2 ought to be enough to indicate the monogamous nature of marriage, Christ leaves no room for doubt or dispute by inserting the word "two": the man and his wife, "the *two* shall become one flesh." Marriage involves an intimate union of two people to the exclusion of all others.

Fourthly, marriage is solitary. A husband and wife must stand together, and this means that to a certain extent they must stand apart. The Lord declares that the first step in the marriage process is to *leave* mother and father. This is necessary so that the marriage partners may truly *cling* to each other. There must be no staying home with, or running home to, the parents. Old relationships must be broken so that the new may be embraced. Marriage involves two people setting out in life together, relying primarily upon each other for their desires and needs.

Fifthly, marriage is permanent. It is a union for life. Once a man and a woman become one flesh, they can never entirely separate themselves again. Their physical union establishes a spiritual union that affects their whole lives. They are spliced together, and cannot be separated without ongoing emotional and mental violence. In addition to this, the Lord Jesus reveals that it is God himself who actually unites a man and a woman in marriage; and he does so with a view to a life-long relationship. *What therefore God has joined together, let not man put asunder!* Marriage involves a commitment from each partner to the other as long as they both live.

Sixthly, marriage is sacred. It is no mere human invention: it is a divine institution. When they marry, a man and a woman enter into a relationship hallowed by God. He is a party to their marriage. He is a witness to their vows and their intimacies, and he binds them to both. He joins them together. Marriage involves the divine as well as the human, the spiritual as well as the physical, the eternal as well as the temporal.

Shifting from Matthew 19 to 1 Corinthians 7, a seventh basic truth about the nature of marriage emerges: marriage is restricted. Christians are not free to marry just anyone. They must either marry another Christian or not marry at all. The Holy Spirit declares through the apostle Paul, "A wife is bound to her husband as long as he lives. If the husband dies, she is free to be married to whom she wishes, only in the Lord." This passage reveals both the liberty and the limit of Christians' choices concerning their marriage partners. Christians are *free to marry whoever they wish*, so long as the partners they choose are *in the Lord*. This restriction is reiterated in 2 Corinthians 6:14-15: "Do not be mismated with unbelievers. For what partnership have righteousness and iniquity? Or what fellowship has light with darkness? What accord has Christ with Belial? Or what has a believer in common with an unbeliever?" Marriage ought to involve the union of a man and a woman who stand in like relationship to God.

While a mixed marriage should not be deliberately entered, neither should it be deliberately broken. A Christian who is already married to a non-Christian should remain in the marriage, love and honour the unbelieving partner, and look to God for his or her salvation (*cf* 1 Cor 7:12-16; 1 Pet 3:1-2).

The purpose of marriage

The opening chapters of Genesis reveal four reasons why God instituted marriage.

Two reasons are evident from Genesis 2:18, where the Lord God discloses his motive for creating woman. He said, "It is not good that the man should be alone; I will make him a helper fit for him." From this statement it can be seen that God made human beings male and female for mutual *companionship* and *support*. Sharing a common humanity and God-likeness, men and women are fit companions and helpers for each other, and marriage is the fit environment for their partnership to flourish.

Another reason God instituted marriage is evident from the marriage formula in Genesis 2:24, where it is stated that husband and wife "become one flesh." Marriage is the proper means for the regulation and the liberation of *sexual expression*.

The fourth reason God instituted marriage is evident from Genesis 1:28, where God commands Adam and Eve, "Be fruitful and multiply". Marriage is the proper place for *procreation*. God intended children to be conceived, born and raised in the context of a loving, life-long marriage relationship. Anything less than this is less than ideal.

A fifth reason God instituted marriage is revealed in Ephesians 5:31-32, where Paul says of the husband-wife relationship, "This mystery is a profound one, and I am saying that it refers to Christ and the church". Marriage is an illustration of Christ's relationship with his bride, the church.

There is a time in most marriages (it should never end, but sadly it often does because of our selfishness and self-assertiveness) when the husband and the wife are in love. During that time, physically and emotionally and spiritually the wife's deepest desire is to yield to her husband's desire, and in yielding she experiences a pleasure and a joy and a worth impossible to be had in any other way. This is how it should be, and one day will be, with the church and her Husband. Nothing short of husband-wife love can convey the intimate, passionate, thrilling love that Christ has for his people, and they for him. He is the lover of our souls; and every redeemed soul is feminine to him,[1] experiencing delight and expressing adoration to the degree that it surrenders to him. Marriage is a portrait of a reality deeper and more enduring than itself.

Government in marriage

There must be government in all human affairs, and this is as true of marriage as it is of any other human association. According to Scripture, there is a hierarchy of authority in marriage. Ideally, the husband should be subject to Christ, the wife should be subject to the husband, and the children should be subject to the parents.

"I want you to understand," Paul writes, "that the head of every man is Christ, the head of a woman is her husband, and the head of Christ is God" (1 Cor 11:3). Elsewhere he states: "Wives, be subject to your husbands, as to the Lord. For the husband is the head of the wife as Christ is the head of the church … As the church is subject to Christ, so let wives also be subject in everything to their husbands" (Eph 5:22-24). Writing under the guidance of the same Spirit, Peter concurs with Paul, urging: "wives, be submissive to your husbands" (1 Pet 3:1).

Hostility to such teaching is widespread. However, it arises in part from a misunderstanding of what the Bible means by masculine authority and feminine submission.

Masculine authority in marriage is not arbitrary or absolute. Husbands are not at liberty to act like autocrats because they themselves are under authority—Christ's authority. Therefore they must act towards their wives as Christ requires them to act.

How does Christ require husbands to act? Paul commands: "Husbands, love your wives, as Christ loved the church and gave himself up for her ... Even so husbands should love their wives as their own bodies" (Eph 5:25, 28). Likewise Peter states: "you husbands, live considerately with your wives, bestowing honour on the woman as the weaker sex, since you are joint heirs of the grace of life" (1 Pet 3:7). From these instructions it is clear that a husband's authority must be exercised kindly, considerately, fairly, sacrificially, and lovingly. It is therefore an authority that should be neither imperious for the man nor onerous for the woman. Under this regime, a wife should never have to stand up for her rights, because her husband should never disregard them.

A husband's headship involves not privilege but responsibility, and for this reason many men reject it. The feminist denial of male leadership is in fact welcomed by many men, for far from wanting to dominate, as feminists assert, they simply wish to escape. They wish to escape the responsibility of providing for their families' financial and emotional and spiritual needs. Nothing suits them better than to believe that they have no special role of leadership in the home. The problem in many marriages today is not that men abuse their authority but that they refuse it.

Scripture does not specifically define the nature of feminine submission in marriage. Passages such as Proverbs 31 portray the wife's role as one of dignity, wisdom, strength, initiative and responsibility, so it is plain that submission has nothing to do with being passive and servile. A statement in Ephesians 5:33 touches the heart of the matter: "let the wife see that she respects her husband." A wife should be supportive of her husband, ready to follow his lead, and disposed to defer to him when mutual agreement proves difficult. In short, she should not be resentful or rebellious, but respectful and responsive.

Wives should appreciate that the Lord Jesus himself is the ultimate object of their obedience: "Wives, be subject to your husbands, *as to the Lord*." In yielding to their husbands, wives are in the first instance showing reverence to the Lord Jesus Christ.

Wives should also appreciate that submissiveness is a necessary part of their witness. In Titus 2:3-5 the apostle Paul instructs older women to "train the young women to love their husbands and children, to be sensible, chaste, domestic, kind, and submissive to their husbands, *that the word of God may not be discredited*." The reason women should, among other things, be submissive to their husbands is so that the word of God may not be discredited. For the Christian wife who rejects her husband's leadership demonstrates to those about her that she doubts the truthfulness and the authority of Scripture. She calls into question the teaching that woman was made from and for man (1 Cor 11:8-9). She spurns the example of the holy women like Sarah who willingly obeyed their husbands (1 Pet 3:1-6). She scorns the explicit teaching concerning the roles of men and women in marriage. She even reverses the spiritual blue-print for marriage, which is the headship of Christ over his bride, the church (Eph 5:23-24). These are some of the ways in which wives who disregard or dominate their husbands discredit the word of God, and thereby ruin their witness.

Concerning Christian wives with non-Christian husbands, 1 Peter 3:1-2 declares: "Likewise you wives, be submissive to your husbands, so that some, though they do not obey the word, may be won without a word by the behaviour of their wives, when they see your reverent and chaste behaviour." Willing and glad acceptance of God's order for marriage is a believing wife's most powerful witness to her unbelieving husband. Without proper deference and reverence, her witness will be at best ineffective and at worst destructive.

Notwithstanding all we have considered about the role of headship and submission between husband and wife, it is important to emphasise that marriage is a partnership. Paul prefaces his teaching about the husband-wife relationship in Ephesians 5 with these words: "Be subject to one another out of reverence for Christ." *Be subject to one another!* Wifely submission should occur in the context of mutual submission. This means that, without forfeiting his authority, a husband must be considerate of his wife and graciously accommodating to her needs and desires. He must do this both out of love for his wife and out of reverence for Christ.

The essence and the balance of the husband-wife relationship is expressed in Colossians 3:18-19: "Wives, be subject to your husbands, as is fitting in the Lord. Husbands, love your wives, and do not be harsh with them."

Sex in marriage

The Bible teaches that marriage is the place for sex. After leaving their parents and cleaving only to each other, a man and a woman become "one flesh". This is the consummation of their marriage.

Marriage is the place for sex, and it is the exclusive place. Scripture repeatedly and roundly condemns any form of sexual behaviour outside of marriage.

God requires absolute fidelity between husband and wife, as the seventh commandment indicates. "You shall not commit adultery" (Exod 20:14) is merely the negative of "You *shall* be faithful." The commandment against adultery covers our thoughts as well as our acts, as the Lord Jesus makes plain in Matthew 5:27-28: "every one who looks at a woman lustfully has already committed adultery with her in his heart." God requires purity and fidelity in mind as well as body. Among other things, this is a decisive argument against pornography. Further, the commandment against adultery covers pre-marital as well as extra-marital activity. For pre-marital sex is simply infidelity in advance of marriage. Men and women should keep themselves pure for their marriage partners *before* as well as *after* their wedding.

Sex is for marriage; and in the context of marriage, sex is good. It is God's wedding gift to the bride and the groom, and it is for their pleasure, comfort and communion. Proverbs 5:18-19 exhorts husbands, "rejoice in the wife of your youth. As a loving hind and a graceful doe, let her breasts satisfy you at all times; be exhilarated always with her love" (NASB).

There is a notion abroad that the Bible disapproves of sex, especially sex for pleasure. This is utter nonsense. *Let her breasts satisfy you*, Scripture says. But it must be *her* breasts, your own wife's, and not another's. Far from viewing sex as corrupt, Scripture views it as sacred, and therefore as worthy of the strongest possible protection.

While the Bible unreservedly *condemns* sex outside marriage, it unreservedly *commends* sex within marriage. Indeed, it commands husbands and wives to satisfy each other's sexual needs, and expressly forbids them to abstain from sexual intimacy, except by mutual agreement for a short time for a religious purpose. 1 Corinthians 7:3-5 states: "The husband should give to his wife her conjugal rights, and likewise the wife to her husband ... Do not refuse one another except perhaps by agreement for a season, that you may devote yourselves to prayer; but then come together again ..."

Paul offers two reasons why husband and wife should be attentive to each other's sexual needs.

Firstly, having insisted that the husband should give his wife her conjugal rights, and vice versa, Paul goes on (v.4): "For the wife does not rule over her own body, but the husband does; likewise the husband does not rule over his own body, but the wife does." In other words, each spouse has right of access to the other's body, and each has a responsibility to respect the other's right. On their wedding day, a bride and a groom freely give their bodies to each other; and this exchange is ongoing.

Secondly, having made provision for husband and wife to abstain from sexual intimacy for a limited and mutually agreed period, Paul instructs (v.5b), "but then come together again, lest Satan tempt you through lack of self-control." Sexual desire cannot be satisfied once, then forgotten. It keeps on asserting itself. Consequently, prolonged abstinence can make a person more susceptible to seduction. A husband and wife have a responsibility to help each other resist sexual temptation by giving each other sexual satisfaction.

Acknowledging each other's rights and helping each other to resist temptation are important but negative reasons for sexual union in marriage. Positive reasons include devotion, adoration and desire. Scripture exalts these in the Song of Songs where, for example, the bridegroom declares (7:6-9):

How fair and pleasant you are,
O loved one, delectable maiden!
You are stately as a palm tree,
and your breasts are like its clusters.
I say I will climb the palm tree
and lay hold of its branches.
Oh, may your breasts be like clusters of the vine,
and the scent of your breath like apples,
and your kisses like the best wine ...

In response the bride declares (7:11-13):

Come, my beloved …
let us go out early to the vineyards …
There I will give you my love.
The mandrakes give forth fragrance,
and over our doors are all choice fruits,
new as well as old,
which I have laid up for you, O my beloved.

Here is a celebration of sex full of sensuality and free of sin, full of gladness and free of guilt, full of pleasure and free of pain, full of delight and free of disease. Here is a holy gift from God, our almighty Creator and Redeemer from whom all blessings flow.

Children in marriage

One of the functions of sex is procreation. Sex may not be *only* for children, but it is *also* for children. And as sex belongs in marriage, so logically children belong in marriage. Scripture simply takes this for granted: marriage is the ideal place for the nurture and upbringing of children.

The Bible reminds us that children are God's gift. The sexual union of husband and wife is merely the means by which the gift of a new life is bestowed. The Creator is behind the procreative act; and it is he, as Psalm 139 points out, who forms the inward parts of the child and knits him together in his mother's womb. Ecclesiastes 11:5 rightly declares that we "do not know how the spirit comes to the bones in the womb of a woman with child". But we *do* know this much: it is "the work of God who makes everything." Therefore, no child is ever a mistake; and no child should ever be murdered in the womb as unwanted.

Psalm 127 states: "Behold, children are a gift of the Lord; the fruit of the womb is a reward. Like arrows in the hand of a warrior, so are the children of one's youth. How blessed is the man whose quiver is full of them" (NASB). Body and soul, children are God's good and gracious gift. They are given for a blessing and a reward.

With this blessing God gives responsibility. Parents must love and care for their children. This involves, of course, clothing, feeding, comforting and protecting them. However, there are two aspects of parental care that Scripture particularly emphasises. One is discipline, the other is education.

Concerning discipline, the book of Proverbs contains much wise advice. It teaches that discipline is an essential part of love. Proverbs 13:24 states, "He who spares the rod hates his son, but he who loves him is diligent to discipline him." Children who are not restrained from doing wrong cause harm even to themselves. As no loving parents want their children to be harmed, all loving parents should discipline their children. A failure to do so is a failure of love. Proverbs 19:18 states, "Discipline your son while there is hope; do not set your heart on his destruction." Discipline must sometimes involve corporal punishment; and while this is regrettable, it is not as terrible as some sensitive people try to make out. Proverbs 23:13-14 declares, "Do not withhold discipline from a child; if you beat him with a rod, he will not die. If you beat him with the rod you will save his life from Sheol." Proverbs 29:15 states, "The rod and reproof give wisdom, but a child left to himself brings shame to his mother." Firm, consistent, loving discipline benefits not only the child but also the whole family. For a rude, selfish, rebellious child causes great stress to all around him. Proverbs 29:17 states, "Discipline your son, and he will give you rest; he will give delight to your heart."

Concerning education, Scripture allocates a special role to parents in the area of values and faith. Parents should diligently seize every opportunity to teach their children about spiritual realities, as is evident from Deuteronomy 6:4-7: "Hear, O Israel: The Lord our God is one Lord; and you shall love the Lord your God with all your heart, and with all your soul, and with all your might. And these words which I command you this day shall be upon your heart; and you shall teach them diligently to your children, and shall talk of them when you sit in your house, and when you walk by the way, and when you lie down, and when you rise."

Religious education is an important duty of parents. Fathers have a special responsibility in this regard, as indicated by the exhortation of Ephesians 6:4: "Fathers, do not provoke your children to anger, but bring them up in the discipline and instruction of the Lord." However, mothers are equally influential, as the example of Eunice demonstrates. She passed on her faith to her son, Timothy; and she did this by ensuring that "from childhood" he was "acquainted with the sacred writings which [were] able to instruct [him] for salvation through faith in Christ Jesus" (2 Tim 3:15). Proverbs 6:20-22 reveals the role of both parents concerning the education of their children: "My son, keep your father's commandment, and forsake not your mother's teaching. Bind them upon your heart always; tie them about your neck. When you walk, they will lead you; when you lie down, they will watch over you; and when you awake, they will talk with you." Both parents have a responsibility to share their faith by word and by example, so that their children might see "the light of the gospel of the glory of Christ, who is the image of God" (2 Cor 4:4; NASB).

Conclusion

Having made us male and female, God instituted marriage for the proper expression and exploration of our masculinity and femininity. To enjoy marriage as God intended we must live it as he instructed. This is the way to bring gladness to our hearts and glory to our God.

The Origin of Fatherhood

On Father's Day my children gave me a card that said on the cover, "Happy Father's Day, Dad. You know this family just wouldn't be the same without you …" I was touched. I began to feel all choked up—until I opened the card and read, "But hey, who wants to live in a normal family anyway!"

My children were joking, of course! But these days such jokes tend to make fathers a little nervous.

In many respects, fatherhood is not held in high esteem in our society today. Fathers are viewed in some quarters as an irrelevance or a nuisance or even a danger, so far as the upbringing of children is concerned. A newspaper article on artificial insemination illustrates the point. The writer states:

> More women are turning to artificial insemination by donor (AID) as a method of conceiving a child. And not just lesbians. A study carried out in Perth last year showed that heterosexual women also were having babies by this method.
>
> The main reason was that they wanted to rear a child, or children, without any interference from a father. They were independent women who sought the freedom to do things in their own way, and AID provided the solution. There was no contact with the father, no custody claims, no child-rearing clashes, visitation rights or any conflict whatsoever. Legally, he simply did not exist.[1]

Apparently, these "independent women" are so determined to avoid "any interference from a father" that they are prepared to be artificially inseminated like cows. There can hardly be a stronger rejection of fathers and fatherhood than that!

In some feminist and sociological circles there is talk about the New Father model. The whole thrust of this model is to strip fathers of all masculine characteristics so they will be just like mothers. New Father visionaries "grimace about maleness". They want fathers to be androgynous, genderless. They want to redefine fatherhood so that it is indistinguishable from motherhood. Indeed, they speak of "co-ed mothering"; and ask earnestly, "Can a man and a woman mother together?" At heart, they believe that "there is nothing special about a father, that there are no fundamental tasks in family life that are properly and necessarily his work." Consequently, it hardly matters whether fathers stick around or not. But if they do, they had better behave like mothers, or else!²

How should Christians respond to such hostility to fathers and fatherhood? One way could be to explore the specific duties that a father has in relation to his children, such as the duty to provide, to protect, to direct, and to discipline. However, I believe our initial response should focus on a more basic issue. Ultimately, the only way to counter claims that fatherhood has no intrinsic reality or worth is to reflect on what the Bible has to say about the origin of fatherhood. Through its many allusions and instructions to fathers, the Bible makes it plain that fatherhood is a reality that involves an identity and a function quite distinct from motherhood. But where does this reality come from? What is the source, the origin, of fatherhood? The Bible offers an astonishing answer to this question.

The apostle Paul states in Ephesians 3:14-15, "I kneel before the Father, from whom all fatherhood in heaven and on earth derives its name."* The reference to "all fatherhood" is a reference to the ideal and practice of fatherhood in families everywhere. Human fatherhood takes its reality from God the Father. He gives his name and nature to it. He is "the Father of all fatherhoods".³ Indeed, "the very notion of fatherhood is derived from the Fatherhood of God."⁴

Where does human fatherhood come from? It comes from God the Father! He is the originator of fatherhood in human society. He is the Father of all fathers. He defines and dignifies human fathers by reference to himself.

Fatherhood originates from God because he is the Original Father. Such a thought leads us into the very depths of the Godhead, and gives us an insight into why the Father is called "the Father". He is not named "the Father" because we humans needed some way of representing him, and fatherhood is the imagery we happened to settle on. Nor does he bear the title because he acts in a fatherly way towards his creation. Rather, the primary reason the first Person of the Trinity is called the Father is because he has a Son. The Father is the Father because of the Son.

The thing that defines someone as a father is a child. A man cannot be a father apart from a child. Fatherhood is a reality that arises from a relationship. A man is a father by virtue of his relationship to and with a son or a daughter. In the same way, God is the Father because of the Son. From all eternity the Father has shared an intimate, paternal relationship with his Son, the Lord Jesus Christ. And he takes his name from that relationship.

The relationship between the first two persons of the Godhead is a Father-Son relationship. It is a *family* relationship. And it is this relationship that underlies the concept and gives rise to the reality not only of "all fatherhood", but also of "every family" (NASB) in heaven and on earth. To the extent that it is a family, each human family takes after the Divine Family. All families get their legitimacy from the Original Family within the Godhead. Along with every father, every family is named after the Father, who himself is named after his relationship with his Son.

It is quite wrong to think that human beings took the initiative to call God "Father". Recently, Oxford University Press published a new translation of the Bible in which God is designated "Father-Mother". One of the thoughts behind this is that by calling God "Father" the Bible expresses the prejudice of its male authors—a prejudice that attributes masculine characteristics to God which do not really belong to him. This masculinisation of God could have been an innocent and inadvertent mistake on the part of the prophets and apostles. But more likely, feminists would have us believe, it came about because the Scriptures were written by men in a patriarchal society who wanted a picture of God that would prop up the illegitimate power of men.

The Holy Spirit speaking with and through Paul in Ephesians 3:14-15 will have none of this. God is not *like* a father: he *is* a father—*the* Father! From all eternity he has been in a Father relationship with his Son. Furthermore, he is not like human fathers: human fathers are, albeit in a limited and imperfect sense, like him. Fathers and fatherhood are named after God, not the other way around.

It is true that God has no gender. He is neither male nor female. Yet it is also true that in his word God reveals himself to us in masculine terms, and teaches us to relate to himself in those terms. And while female imagery is used for God on several occasions in the Bible, nowhere is God ever directly spoken of as Mother or Wife or Queen or Lady. Nowhere ever! He is always and only spoken of as Father and Husband and King and Lord.

Christians should not entertain the view that the masculine portrayals of God in scripture merely reflect the masculine perspectives of the writers. Such a view is a direct attack on the inspiration of God's word. It leads us to believe that the prophets and apostles were not after all holy and honourable men who wrote as the Holy Spirit directed them, but rather were men who could not see past their own patriarchal society and sexist prejudices. We dare not think such things about the men through whom God communicated his infallible word.

The apostle Peter states that "no prophecy of Scripture came about by the prophet's own interpretation. For prophecy never had its origin in the will of man, but men spoke from God as they were carried along by the Holy Spirit" (2 Pet 1:20-21, NIV). So then, if the Holy Spirit had moved the prophets and apostles to describe God as Mother, they would have done so. But he did not. He inspired them to view him and to reveal him as Father. If this is not true then it is an argument not to alter but to abolish the Bible. For if God did not speak truthfully and meaningfully when he revealed himself to us as Father and Husband and King and Lord, then why should we believe he has spoken truthfully and meaningfully in other matters?

While not denying that the Father imagery for God is inspired, some Christians maintain that it is nonetheless inappropriate imagery for contemporary society. "There are many bad fathers about," they reason, "and fatherhood has fallen into disrepute. So it is no longer tenable to speak of God as 'Father'. This title simply alienates people." There are several errors in this type of reasoning.

Firstly, while some fathers are bad, there are not nearly as many bad fathers as feminists, therapists and journalists would have us believe. Many fathers are good, while many more are in between, caring for their children acceptably though not outstandingly. We should not uncritically accept the bad press given to fathers today, let alone revise our beliefs and behaviours in the light of it.

Secondly, we should not allow the existence of the bad to overshadow the existence of the good. There *are* good earthly fathers, and there *is* a good heavenly Father. These good models should govern our view of fatherhood, not the bad models. We should not fall silent about the good just because others are shouting about the bad. As Paul admonishes in Romans 12:21, "Do not be overcome by evil, but overcome evil with good."

Thirdly, we should encourage those who have had a bad experience of fatherhood to realise that it is possible to have a good experience of fatherhood. We must help the young man with a bad father to see that he need not be a bad father himself. We must help the young woman with a bad father to see that the father of her children need not be bad. People harmed by a bad relationship with a father need more than anyone else to be reassured that a good relationship with a human father is possible.

Fourthly, we should encourage those who have had a bad earthly father to see that they can have a good heavenly Father. Such people need a father whom they can trust, and God is such a Father. He will be a true Father to them. And as they experience his loving fatherhood, they will also experience healing from the wounds inflicted by an unloving fatherhood. Those who have been hurt or abandoned by a human father do not need us to apologise because Jesus and the apostles portray God as "Father". On the contrary, they need us to tell them that this good and loving Father can be their Father, too. What better news can we give to the emotional orphan than to tell him or her that God delights to be "a father to the fatherless" (Ps 68:5, NIV)?

When we appreciate that the Father is the One from whom all fatherhood flows, we begin to appreciate that the name "Father" is not an arbitrary title for God. We also begin to appreciate that fatherhood is not an arbitrary state for men. Fatherhood is not merely a human construct, a human invention. The proponents of the New Father model, as already noted, want to destroy all gender-based parental roles. They ignore or deny all biological, emotional and intellectual differences between men and women. They strive to turn fathers into mothers. They want to take the masculinity out of fatherhood. And they think they are free to do this because they think that fatherhood is both unimportant and arbitrary. But they are wrong.

Fatherhood *is* important and it is *not* arbitrary. It is not something we have constructed: it is something that has been constructed for us. It cannot be done away with or altered at a whim because God gives his name and his nature to it. Fatherhood derives its existence and its function from the Father. Consequently, it must be viewed and practised with respect. We are not free to minimise or modify it to suit ourselves. On the contrary, we are under an obligation to discover its true purpose and its best expression. To do this, we must ponder the instructions and insights God offers to fathers in his holy word. And we must look to the Father himself and examine his fatherly relationship with both his eternal Son and his adopted children.

Indeed, we human fathers need to become personally acquainted with the divine Father. Such an acquaintance can be arranged by God's Son, Jesus Christ. He said, "no one knows the Father except the Son and anyone to whom the Son chooses to reveal him" (Matt 11:27). And he chooses to reveal the Father to everyone who approaches him in repentance and faith.

The Father is the foundation of our fatherhood. Only he can give enduring meaning and dignity to our nature and role as fathers. Only he can supply adequate strength and wisdom to help us to discharge our paternal duties. Only he can give ultimate meaning to our children as they see his love and authority in us.

With Paul, then, let us kneel before the Father, from whom all fatherhood and every father in heaven and on earth is named.

---

* The subtleties of the Greek text allow several variations of meaning. This translation is found in the margin, or footnote, of the New International Version.

The main text of the New International Version renders Paul's statement: "I kneel before the Father, from whom *his whole family* in heaven and on earth derives its name". Translated this way, the reference to the *whole family* is a reference to all Christians who, having become the children of God by faith, constitute the family of God by adoption. In heaven and on earth, believers are named as a family by virtue of their relationship with God as their Father. Such a thought is true, but it is probably not the truth foremost in Paul's mind on this occasion.

The New American Standard Bible translates Paul's statement: "I bow my knees before the Father, from whom *every family* in heaven and on earth derives its name". Translated this way, the reference to *every family* is a reference to every group throughout the world that is headed by a father. All such groups are named and modelled after God the Father, who from eternity has been in a family relationship with the Son.

The First Duty of Fatherhood

A man cannot be a father without a woman, and he should not be a father without a wedding. This is why in Ephesians the apostle Paul does not address fathers until he has first addressed husbands and wives. He begins, "Wives, be subject to your husbands". He adds, "Husbands, love your wives". He continues, "Children, obey your parents". He concludes, "Fathers, do not provoke your children to anger, but bring them up in the discipline and instruction of the Lord."

A family begins, or ought to begin, with a man and a woman who are morally and legally united as husband and wife. It is within this context that sex is enjoyed and children are born. The husband-wife relationship is the foundation of the father-child relationship.

When we understand this, we begin to understand that the duties of a father are bound up with the duties of a husband. And what are the duties of a husband? They can be summarised in these terms: "Husbands, love your wives, as Christ loved the church and gave himself up for her" (Eph 5:25). Husband, love your wife tenderly, as Christ loves the church. Love her passionately, as Christ loves the church. Love her sacrificially, as Christ loves the church. Love her forgivingly, as Christ loves the church. Love her patiently, as Christ loves the church. Love her enduringly, as Christ loves the church. Love her unconditionally, as Christ loves the church. Love her!

The first duty of a father is to love and cherish the mother of his children. If he wants the best for his children, then he must seek the best for his wife, because their welfare is inextricably linked with hers.

In order to provide for his children, a man must first provide for his wife. While the children are young and dependent upon their mother, it is a father's duty to earn the family income. This stands to reason when we consider the constraints placed on a mother by pregnancy, childbirth, nursing and nurturing. A woman cannot carry on all her former activities during these times. She is physically unable to do so. Her husband has an obligation to meet her needs during these times so that she can meet their children's needs.

While women rightly take their place in the paid workforce, they should not be expected to continue outside employment when they become mothers. Of course, some women may be compelled to go back to work for financial reasons, while others may desire to go back for personal or professional reasons. In agreement with their husbands, let such women do what their needs or aspirations demand and their consciences permit. But many women do *not* want to go back to work. On entering motherhood, they desire to leave paid employment to devote themselves to their children. These women should not be forced back into the workplace. Their desires should be respected by all, especially their husbands.

Fathers should provide mothers with the opportunity to mother their children. Infants need constant and intimate care; and the person best suited to give that care is the mother. While other people can stand in temporarily, no one but the mother can discharge the duty entirely—not even the father.

Writing in *Quadrant* magazine, Anne Manne describes in deeply moving terms how and why she chose to set aside her career as a university lecturer and researcher in order to care for her children over the first dozen or so years of their lives. She states:

> Many women, distinguished, homely, exceptional and ordinary, often describe the process of bonding [between mother and child] as a kind of "falling in love" …
>
> When I considered going back to work, it was not only that my children, having not read the equal opportunity handbook in the womb, had other ideas. It was also that my priorities changed. … what had seemed a reasonable course of action before birth—using daycare—now seemed unthinkable in relation to this tiny human being …
>
> When I worked one day a week after the first few months, leaving

our baby in the care of her father, although I found the morning a welcome break … by the afternoon I was gripped by feelings of anguish, experiencing an overwhelming desire to be with my baby. We would come together again into one another's safekeeping with the pleasure and intensity of lovers. If my children's instinct was to keep me close, mine was to keep them close.[1]

Fathers need to recognise that mothers have an overwhelming desire to be with their children and to keep them close. This is a mother's God-given instinct. And a father's responsibility is to ensure that this instinct, this desire, can be fulfilled. He must provide a stable environment for his wife to lavish love on the children, for her own well-being and for theirs.

Generally speaking, when a woman becomes a mother, her priorities change. This change should be acknowledged and honoured. Indeed, if we are to treat men and women with equal respect, we must respect the different ways in which men and women experience parenthood. Motherhood is not the same as fatherhood. And one of the functions of fatherhood is to ensure that motherhood can be practised with joy and devotion.

There is a pressing need in our society to provide mothers with the opportunity to mother. Recognising this need, a man should not put pressure on his wife to return to paid employment after childbirth. Rather, he should acknowledge the special bond between mother and child and do all in his power to preserve and strengthen that bond. This will require him to be the family's "sole bread winner"—a role which is often misrepresented as chauvinistic, but which in fact involves sacrificial love deserving of high praise.

In the process of providing his wife with the opportunity to mother their children, a husband must also protect her against influences that are hostile or harmful to family life. One such influence is feminism, which has fostered widespread prejudice in our society against women who choose to make a vocation of motherhood.

Feminists would have us believe that motherhood does not—and certainly should not—make much difference to the way a woman feels and thinks. They deliberately empty the mother-child relationship of its meaning by describing it as the "home based provision of such services as child care". One prominent

Australian feminist, Eva Cox, has "likened caring for children to such leisure activities as making jam".[2] Eva Cox has also allegedly stated that "Any mother who is not back in the workplace when her child is 12 months old is a bludger on society."[3] This contempt by feminists for motherhood is nothing short of a contempt for women. And many mothers today suffer a dreadful loss of self-esteem because of it.

The noxious influence of feminism is so pervasive in modern society that, according to Anne Manne, women who spend time out of the workforce

> often experience social shame in being "just a mother". The media, particularly, over-represented as it is by career women, not only continually overstates the number of women in the workforce with young children, but also gives a strong sense that to get out of [the workforce] is to be a social fossil. It is our generation's version of being "left on the shelf". ... And it is a peculiarity of modern times that the woman who looks after someone else's children has more social approval than the woman who looks after her own. Recently, a friend met a woman who, heavily pregnant, told her of her plans to go back to work straight away. The task of looking after [a baby], changing and washing all those nappies was too humdrum for her, she said. What was her occupation, my friend enquired? A hospital orderly—you know, the ones who change the babies' nappies in the nursery, while the mothers rest![1]

"For my own part," Manne continues, "it was amusing to notice that while I have worked at all kinds of jobs ... I have never received the kind of social disapproval, particularly from the elite, for any of those jobs, that I have experienced in looking after [my] young children."

Manne rightly points out that, thanks to feminism, child-rearing has come to be regarded "as an obstacle to [a woman's] fulfilment, and the child as a kind of nuisance, preventing participation in the main game." To illustrate this sad fact, she recorded the following anecdote:

> At a child's birthday party recently I listened to a conversation between two women home with, between them, six children under five. Their

children are a credit to both of them. They were talking to a career woman with one child who had spent his life since a few weeks old in childcare full-time … The inevitable question came: "What do you do?" "I have my own office," she replied, with great pride. The other women looked abashed. "I don't do *anything* really," said one. But then she brightened. "I do try to get to the gym a few times a week." The other just looked defensive and spoke of her intention to go back to work "soon". They were *ashamed* of themselves. A slow smile of superiority slid across the face of the career woman.

Though it is unlikely that they will ever work harder in their lives, and though little "work" could be more important, they felt themselves to be *doing nothing*. We now live with a frame of values in which what these women are doing has become invisible even to themselves.[2]

Husbands have a duty to protect their wives from the social disapproval generated by feminism against women who devote themselves to mothering. Mothers in the home are suffering a tremendous assault on their own sense of dignity and worth. A husband should support his wife in her work, encouraging her to see the value of her role as a mother, and boosting her self-esteem. A father can do no better by his children than to affirm the value of their mother.

A man cannot love his children well without prizing their mother highly. This, then, is his first duty as a father. Or to put it another way: The first duty of fatherhood is to facilitate motherhood. First and foremost, a father should provide for and protect the mother of his children. By doing this he will enable her to nurture their children in a way that gives both her and them security, satisfaction and self-respect.

The High King's Watchmen

God has given his people the privilege and responsibility to be watchmen for the communities and nations in which they live. The role of the spiritual watchman is outlined in Ezekiel 3:16-19 (*cf* 33:1-9):

> the word of the Lord came to me: "Son of man, I have made you a watchman for the house of Israel; whenever you hear a word from my mouth, you shall give them warning from me. If I say to the wicked, 'You shall surely die,' and you give him no warning, nor speak to warn the wicked from his wicked way, in order to save his life, that wicked man shall die in his iniquity; but his blood I will require at your hand. But if you warn the wicked, and he does not turn from his wickedness, or from his wicked way, he shall die in his iniquity; but you will have saved your life."

God called Ezekiel to be a watchman. Ezekiel did not have any choice in the matter. The Lord said, "I have made you a watchman". I believe this is true of every Christian. Whether we like it or not, God has made us his watchmen, his watchwomen. We can choose to obey or to disobey, but we cannot choose to be other than what God has made us. We *are* the High King's watchmen.

Having commissioned Ezekiel, the Lord told him the duties he was to perform and the message he was to proclaim: you must warn them "whenever you hear a word from my mouth". Evidently, Ezekiel received direct communications from the Lord. He knew exactly when the Lord spoke and he knew exactly what the Lord spoke (*cf* 1:1, 3, 28; 2:2; 3:12, 22, 24).

To be watchmen, we too must hear the Lord speak and the Bible enables us to do this. The Bible is the Word of God in written form, out-breathed by the Holy Spirit through the prophets and apostles, and "profitable for teaching, for reproof, for correction, and for training in righteousness" (2 Tim 3:16; *cf* 2 Pet 1:19-21). What God spoke to Ezekiel and the other prophets and apostles he still speaks. The word he gave to them he gives to us.

If we read the Bible diligently, the Spirit of God who inspired it will enlighten our minds to understand it (1 Cor 2:12-16). And as the Word of God becomes living and active in our hearts and minds, it will instruct us concerning what to believe and how to behave. It will speak to our personal needs and to our society's needs. It will give us (among other things) a word from the Lord with which to warn those who are in danger.

According to Ezekiel, the message that the watchman is to give is a word of warning. The warning, in essence, is that God is not mocked (Gal 6:7). He will not tolerate sin. On the contrary, he is coming to bring judgment. The watchman must warn the wicked, "You shall surely die" (3:18).

Through Ezekiel, through the watchman, the Lord warns that those guilty of adultery, idolatry, robbery, cruelty, greed, injury, injustice, *et cetera*, are facing judgment; and when that judgment is pronounced it will bring death: "The soul that sins shall die" (18:4, 20).

The watchman's message, then, is by nature a warning that God's condemnation awaits those who disobey him. But what is its purpose? Is the watchman to tell the wicked that they "shall surely die" simply to terrify them? No, not at all! Although terror may be a function of the warning, it is not its primary purpose.

The watchman must "speak to warn the wicked from his wicked way, *in order* to save his life" (3:18). With God, warnings are for turnings. His warnings are deterrents, not determinations; they are cautions, not causations. Hence, the purpose of the watchman's warning is to bring the wicked to repentance so that they might obtain deliverance.

In Ezekiel 18, the Lord asks, "Have I any pleasure in the death of the wicked ... and not rather that he should turn from his way and live?" (v 23). Later in the same chapter he declares, "For I have no pleasure in the death of any one ... so turn, and live" (v 32). In chapter 33, he instructs Ezekiel, "Say to them, As I live, says the Lord God, I have no pleasure in the death of the wicked, but that the wicked turn from his way and live". Then he pleads with the wicked directly: "turn back, turn back from your evil ways; for why will you die ... ?" (v 11). It is difficult to read this plea without sensing the compassion (not to mention the frustration and distress) that motivates it. Behold what manner of love the Lord has for the wicked, that he should plead with them in this manner!

We need to remember that the Lord does not wish "that any should perish, but that all should reach repentance" (2 Pet 3:9; cf 1 Tim 2:4). For example, not the liar nor the thief nor the adulterer nor the prostitute nor the homosexual nor the abortionist—not one of these wrongdoers does God wish to be lost. The highest purpose of the watchman's warning is to turn these people from their wickedness so that they might have life, and have it abundantly and eternally.

Faithful watchmen can sometimes find it difficult to battle continually against evil without feeling bitter towards those who glory in it. But we must guard against such bitterness. We must take care not to be like Jonah.

Jonah was troubled by this desire to see the wicked get their just desserts. He proclaimed the warning to the people of Nineveh, "'Yet forty days, and Nineveh shall be overthrown!' And the people of Nineveh believed God; they proclaimed a fast, and put on sackcloth, from the greatest of them to the least of them" (3:4-5). When God saw "how they turned from their evil way", he repented—that is, he changed his mind and abandoned his intention to destroy them. This upset Jonah and he complained, "I pray you, Lord, is not this what I said when I was yet in my country? That is why I made haste to flee to Tarshish; for I knew that you are a gracious God and merciful, slow to anger, and abounding in steadfast love, and repent of evil. Therefore now, O Lord, take my life from me, I beseech you, for it is better for me to die than to live" (4:2-3). He despised the wicked so much that he would rather die than witness their redemption.

Jonah hoped that God would fulfil his warning that Nineveh was to be destroyed in forty days. But God intended that the warning itself would make the destruction unnecessary. It was for love of them that God warned the wicked, "You shall surely die".

It is easy to label people who oppose evil and speak of judgment as "negative", but this is not a biblical view.

The Bible is often couched in "negative" language. It often warns people against sin. It does not simply commend the good; it also condemns the bad. Of the Ten Commandments, for example, only two are expressed positively. The other eight begin with the declaration, "You shall not". This approach is frowned on today. We want to be "positive" about everything. But God insists on being negative—and dogmatic: *You shall not!*

Before people can repent, they have to become aware that they need to repent. To that end, we must sometimes speak "negatively", identifying and condemning sin for what it is.

So the watchman must sometimes warn the wicked with a message that seems wholly negative. But the purpose is primarily positive. "You shall surely die," he warns, in the hope that the wicked might take heed, repent and live.

Both the calling of the watchman and the message he is to deliver come from God. But the delivery of the message is the watchman's responsibility— and he is free to accept or to reject that responsibility (although, as we see in the case of Jonah, God is free to reject his rejection).

If the watchman disobeys God's command to warn the wicked, he is guilty of sin and will be held accountable. But worse, his disobedience may result in the damnation of the wicked. The Lord warns, "If the watchman sees the sword coming and does not blow the trumpet, so that the people are not warned, and the sword comes, and takes any one of them; that man is taken away in his iniquity, but his blood I will require at the watchman's hand" (Ez 33:6; *cf* Acts 20:26-28).

While the watchman has a responsibility to warn, the wicked man has a responsibility to heed the warning. He is challenged to repent. And, like the inhabitants of Nineveh, he *can* repent if he so desires. But he can also choose to ignore the warning and to continue in his evil ways.

If he heeds the warning, he will live. If he ignores it, he will die. The Lord declares, "if anyone who hears the sound of the trumpet does not take warning, and the sword comes and takes him away, his blood shall be upon his own head … But if he had taken warning he would have saved his life" (Ez 33:4-5). Each human being is a moral being and is therefore both responsible for his actions and accountable to God for them. Hence, if he chooses to ignore the warning, he is responsible for his own death.

Furthermore, the wicked man has no excuse *even if the watchman fails to warn.* He had the choice to refrain from wickedness in the first place; and having turned to wickedness, he had the choice to turn back from it. With or without the warning, the wicked man is guilty of sin and is justly condemned. The tragedy is that had he been warned he might have repented and lived. He might have received mercy instead of justice.

We must not make light of our responsibilities as watchmen: the wicked can be lost for want of a warning. God is not dependent on us but in his wisdom he chooses to work through us. Hence, "we are ambassadors for Christ, God making his appeal through us" (2 Cor 5:20).

God has entrusted "to us the message of reconciliation". This message is that "God was in Christ reconciling the world to himself, not counting their trespasses against them" (2 Cor 5:19). In Christ, God acted to restore a right relationship between himself and mankind. He sacrificed his Son so that our sins could be set aside. When we believe in Christ and accept by faith his work on the cross, God does not count our sins against us any more. This is the message of reconciliation with which we have been entrusted.

The gospel is the main message the Lord would have us declare to the world. It is both a word of warning and a word of hope. The Apostle John expresses the dual nature of the gospel message like this: "He who believes in the Son has eternal life; he who does not obey the Son shall not see life, but the wrath of God rests upon him" (John 3:36). The Apostle Paul puts it like this: "For the wages of sin is death, but the free gift of God is eternal life in Christ Jesus our Lord" (Rom 6:23).

The gospel has a positive and a negative side. It is good news for those who believe, but bad news for those who disbelieve (*cf* 2 Cor 2:14-16). The Bible does not shrink from declaring both sides of the gospel message.

However, while the gospel is our first priority, it is not our only concern. We live in a world where deceit, wrongdoing and injustice are daily realities. As watchmen appointed by the Lord, we must sound an alarm against many evils, especially those evils that are accepted or approved by society at large. For example, we should warn against a range of defiling and destructive evils connected with fallen sexual desire, evils such as prostitution, pornography, adultery, pre-marital sex and homosexuality. Warning against such evils will not make us popular, but who will warn the perishing about them if not Christians?

And such warnings serve the gospel. We tend to categorize issues as either social or spiritual, and there can be value in doing this. However, it is wrong to believe that the two categories are mutually exclusive. Social issues are spiritual issues, too. Paul makes this clear when he states, "Do not be deceived: neither the sexually immoral, nor idolaters, nor adulterers, nor men who practice homosexuality … will inherit the kingdom of God" (1 Cor 6:9-10). Sexual sins (to isolate just one kind of sin for the sake of argument) have not only social but also spiritual impact. True, they spread debauchery, jealousy, resentment and disease throughout society and in this way they break down family relationships and social cohesion. But this is not the worst of it. The most dreadful consequence of sexual sin is alienation from God, which, if not reversed, excludes offenders from God's kingdom for eternity.

Sexual immorality is a spiritual as well as a social issue. It is not an issue separate from the gospel but one that relates to it. The same is true for every social evil against which the Christian watchman must warn.

The wicked are not the only ones who can benefit from the watchman's warning. The redeemed can, too. We need to watch out for the Church as well as the world, for evils that flourish in the general community have a way of filtering into the Christian community.

God will bring judgment on the Church if it fails to warn the world against evil practices. And one of the ways his judgment will come is by allowing the Church itself to be harmed by the very evil to which it abandoned the world. In a very real sense, when we watch and warn the godless about evil and judgment, we protect ourselves.

Mordecai pointed this out to Queen Esther when she was afraid to approach the king over the impending destruction of the Jews in Persia. He told her, "Think not that in the king's palace you will escape any more than all the other Jews. For if you keep silence at such a time as this, relief and deliverance will rise for the Jews from another quarter, but you and your father's house will perish. And who knows whether you have not come to the kingdom for such a time as this?" (Est 4:13-14). Essentially, Mordecai is saying, "Don't think you'll escape when the evil day comes. You won't escape unscathed. There's nowhere that's safe, not even the king's palace. Do something! Do what you know is right! It just may be that you are the one God has raised up to save us!" May God grant us wisdom and courage to heed the warning of Mordecai and to follow the example of Esther! For who knows whether we have not come to our nation for such a time as this?

As Christians, we are called to social action.

In Matthew 5:13, our Lord declares, "You are the salt of the earth". What are the qualities of salt? It heals wounds. It preserves from decay. It enhances flavour. It stimulates thirst. Whether we like it or not, we *are* the salt of the earth. The question is: Are we healing, preserving, seasoning and stimulating our society, or have we lost our saltiness?

In Matthew 5:14, our Lord declares, "You are the light of the world". What are the qualities of light? It overcomes darkness. It shines brighter as the night gets darker. It reveals hidden things. It makes plain the path we must tread. Whether we like it or not, we *are* the light of the world. The question is: Are we shining on top of a lampstand or under a basket?

In Ezekiel 3:16, our Lord declares, "I have made you a watchman for the house of Israel". What are the responsibilities of the watchman? He must watch vigilantly. He must detect the movements of the enemy. He must warn his fellows of approaching danger. Whether we like it or not, we *are* the watchmen for our nation. The question is: Are we at our posts or at our pleasures?

We are the Lord's lookouts. We are the High King's watchmen. We will not all look in the same direction or look after the same people. We each have our own wall to watch and our own community to warn. Let us be faithful in this.

Isaiah said of the priests of Israel, the "watchmen are blind, they are all without knowledge; they are all dumb dogs, they cannot bark; dreaming, lying down, loving to slumber" (56:10). May this never be said of Christians today. Rather, may it be said of us as it was said of Nehemiah's workmen, "Each of the builders had his sword girded at his side while he built" (Neh 4:18). May we always have "the sword of the Spirit, which is the word of God" (Eph 6:17), strapped to our sides as we strive to build the kingdom of God until the King of Glory comes.

Social & Moral Concerns

A Biblical Perspective Abortion

The Bible does not contain any direct teaching on abortion. So to learn God's view on this matter, we need to determine what his word says on two related matters. Firstly, we need to know what it says about the nature of prenatal life. Secondly, we need to know what it says about the value of human life.

The nature of prenatal life

We can deduce the nature of prenatal life from the many references in the Bible to conception, pregnancy and birth.

To begin with, the Bible clearly portrays prenatal life as human life. God's word identifies the unborn as children. A pregnant woman does not carry a cluster of cells that could become a child. She carries a *child*.

Rom 9:10 states, for example, that Rebecca "conceived children" by Isaac. According to Genesis 25:22, "The children struggled together within her". Hosea 12:3 states that "In the womb [Jacob] took his brother by the heel", while Genesis 25:26 indicates that Jacob still had hold of Esau's heel when they were born! Distressed by the antics of her unborn children, Rebecca "went to enquire of the Lord. And the Lord said to her, 'Two nations are in your womb, and two peoples, born of you, shall be divided; the one shall be stronger than the other, the elder shall serve the younger'" (25:22-23). The behaviour of the foetuses, as well as the Lord's explanation for that behaviour, plainly indicates their humanity. *Before birth* Esau and Jacob were children, twin brothers, who had distinct characters and destinies.

To be pregnant means to be "with child". Translations such as the King James Version and the Revised Standard Version bring this out. For example, the angel of the Lord tells Hagar in Genesis 16:11 "Behold, you are with child, and shall bear a son; you shall call his name Ishmael". In 1 Samuel 4:19 we read, "the wife of Phinehas, was with child, about to give birth." Concerning David's adultery with Bathsheba, 2 Samuel 11:5 states, "And the woman conceived; and she sent and told David, 'I am with child.'"

In the New Testament, the same Greek word is used to speak of a child before and after birth. According to the context in which it appears, the word *brephos* means either an unborn child or a newborn child. For example, Luke 1:41 states that "the babe [John] leaped in [Elizabeth's] womb" (*cf* v.44), while Luke 2:16 states that the shepherds found "the babe [Jesus] lying in a manger" (*cf* v.12). The same word, *brephos*, is used to describe John as an unborn baby and Jesus as a newborn baby. The Bible makes no distinction between the two. This is because a child does not become something different after he is born: he is the same being before birth as after birth—all that has changed (and will go on changing) is his level of maturity.

The clearest portrayal of the humanity of the unborn in the Bible is found in Luke's account of the conceptions and prenatal lives of John and Jesus. Luke records that after Mary had conceived the Lord Jesus, she "went with haste" (1:39) to see Elizabeth, who was six months pregnant (1:36) with the prophet John. Luke continues: "And when Elizabeth heard the greeting of Mary, the babe leaped in her womb; and Elizabeth was filled with the Holy Spirit and she exclaimed with a loud cry, 'Blessed are you among women, and blessed is the fruit of your womb! And why is this granted me, that the mother of my Lord should come to me? For behold, when the voice of your greeting came to my ears, the babe in my womb leaped for joy'" (1:41-44). John was a six-month-old foetus when he recognised the person and rejoiced at the presence of the Lord Jesus Christ in the womb of Mary. More significantly, Jesus was only a several-day-old embryo at that time.

Jesus assumed our humanity at conception. He began his human existence as an embryo and a foetus. Within days of his conception, he was hailed by Elizabeth as "Lord" and greeted by John with joy.

According to scripture, prenatal life is human life.

The Bible also indicates that prenatal life is human life *from conception*. Conception is the point at which human life commences. Genesis 4:1 states, for example, "Adam knew Eve his wife, and she conceived and bore Cain, saying, 'I have gotten a man with the help of the LORD.'" When did Eve get her man-child, Cain? Scripture makes it clear that she got him at conception. She gave birth to him because she conceived him and carried him in her womb. Cain came into existence at conception, not birth. There is no thought in scripture that the unborn Cain was somehow different from the newborn Cain. Nor is there any hint that the first-trimester Cain was somehow different from the second- or third-trimester Cain. They were one and the same. Cain was Cain from conception. That is when his life began as a human being.

Dozens of similar passages cite conception as the beginning of human life. For example, Genesis 4:17 states, "Cain knew his wife, and she conceived and bore Enoch". Genesis 21:2 states, "Sarah conceived, and bore Abraham a son". Genesis 29:32 states, "Leah conceived and bore a son". 1 Samuel 1:20 states, "Hannah conceived and bore a son". These and many similar statements tie the origin of human life to conception. In fact, because scripture places such weight on conception as the starting point of human life, it often begins the narrative of a person's life by referring to the sexual act that resulted in his or her conception: "*Adam knew Eve his wife*, and she conceived and bore Cain"; "*Cain knew his wife*, and she conceived and bore Enoch".

Job traces the beginning of his existence back beyond his birth to his conception. At the height of his suffering he wished that he had never lived, declaring, "Let the day perish wherein I was born, and the night which said, 'A man-child is conceived'" (3:3). Job understood that his life began on the night he was conceived.

Jeremiah understood this, too. Like Job, he went through a time of such suffering and despair that he longed for oblivion. But while Job wished he had never been conceived, Jeremiah wished he had been aborted. He cried, "Cursed be the day on which I was born! ... Cursed be the man who brought the news to my father, 'A son is born to you,' making him very glad. Let that man be [cursed] ... because he did not kill me in the womb; so my mother would have been my grave" (Jer 20:14-17). Note Jeremiah's expression, "kill me in the womb". If the man who announced Jeremiah's birth had performed an abortion on Jeremiah's mother, *Jeremiah* would have been *killed*. That man would not have "eliminated" the unwanted "products of conception". He would have *killed* a unique *human being*.

According to scripture, prenatal life is human life; and it is human life from conception.

Further, the Bible teaches that from conception human life is created and coddled by God. David reveals in Psalm 139:13-16 that God takes an active part in the formation of human life within the womb. He declares, "you created my inmost being; you knit me together in my mother's womb. I praise you because I am fearfully and wonderfully made ... My frame was not hidden from you when I was made in the secret place. ... All the days ordained for me were written in your book before one of them came to be" (NIV). God did not create a biological organism within the womb that became David at birth. Rather, he created *David himself*. In an awesome and wonderful way, God wove together David's "frame" and his "inmost being" in "the secret place" of his mother's womb, all the while seeing David's life as a unified entity, a vital continuum from conception to old age.

Like David, Job acknowledges that God formed him—and indeed forms every human being—in the womb. Referring to himself and his servants, Job states, "Did not [God] who made me in the womb make them? Did not the same one form us both within our mothers?" (Job 31:15, NIV).

Jeremiah makes a claim similar to Job's and David's when he says, "Now the word of the Lord came to me saying, 'Before I formed you in the womb I knew you, and before you were born I consecrated you; I appointed you a prophet to the nations'" (1:4-5). A fascinating thing about the Lord's word to Jeremiah is that it indicates that Jeremiah's life began, in a sense, even before conception. It originated in the consciousness of God, so that conception was simply the confirmation of God's intention concerning Jeremiah's coming-into-being. But that is another matter. The significant thing so far as the matter of abortion is concerned is God's assertion, "I formed you in the womb".

God is intimately involved in the creation of human life from conception. A man and a woman are essentially the vehicles through which a new person comes into existence: the actual creation of that person is God's work from beginning to end. It is the Lord "who gives breath to the people upon [the earth] and spirit to those who walk in it" (Isa 42:5). Ecclesiastes 11:5 states, "As you do not know how the spirit comes to the bones in the womb of a woman with child, so you do not know the work of God who makes everything." We do not and cannot know how God forms a living soul from the union of a sperm and an ovum—but he does!

David, Job, Jeremiah—each acknowledges that his human existence began before birth, and that God was intimately involved in the creation of his existence.

The value of human life

Prenatal life is by nature human life, human life fashioned by God from conception. So to determine the value of this life, we must simply determine the value of human life.

The Bible presents six truths about human life that establish its value.

Firstly, God created human life. Genesis 2:7 states, "the LORD God formed man of dust from the ground, and breathed into his nostrils the breath of life; and man became a living being."

Secondly, God bestowed his own nature on human life. Genesis 1:27 states, "God created man in his own image, in the image of God he created him; male and female he created them."

Thirdly, God owns human life. In Ezekiel 18:4 the Lord states, "Behold, all souls are mine".

Fourthly, God preserves human life. Acts 17:25 states that God "himself gives to all men life and breath and everything".

Fifthly, God values human life. The Lord Jesus declares in Matthew 10:29-31, "Are not two sparrows sold for a penny? And not one of them will fall to the ground without your Father's will ... Fear not, therefore; you are of more value than many sparrows."

Sixthly, God forbids the wilful, unlawful destruction of human life. Exod 20:13 states, "You shall not murder." Indeed, foremost among the "things which the LORD hates" are "hands that shed innocent blood" (Prov 6:16-17).

In summary, the Bible asserts that human life has inestimable worth. It is precious beyond calculation because it is created, distinguished, sustained, owned and treasured by God himself, who utterly forbids its wanton destruction.

Conclusion

Scripture leads us to believe that prenatal life is human life and that human life is immensely precious. Working from these two facts, we can deduce a third fact: prenatal life is immensely precious. Our reasoning is as follows: If a foetus is a human being, and if a human being is invaluable, then a foetus is invaluable.

What does this tell us about abortion, then? The logic is inescapable. If abortion kills a foetus, and if a foetus is a human being, then abortion kills a human being. And if God abhors the destruction of innocent human life, and if a foetus is an innocent human life, then God abhors the destruction of a foetus by abortion.

From a scriptural standpoint, there is no ambiguity about the moral nature of abortion. It is a monstrous evil that destroys God's handiwork, defies his purpose and denies his love. It is the deliberate, despicable killing of an innocent, helpless human being for the convenience of a mother (not to mention a father) and the profit of a doctor.

Without doubt, God looks upon such killings with outrage. The children who are aborted are not hidden from him. He sees their little bodies as they are torn apart. He hears their silent screams. The darkness of the womb is as light to him, and he will bring into judgment the secret things that happen there.

As for God's people, we must do more than merely abstain from abortion ourselves. We must condemn the practice with vigour. We must strive to save the unborn children who are under threat. Solomon exhorts and warns in Proverbs 24:10-12:

> If you faint in the day of adversity, your strength is small. Rescue those who are being taken away to death; hold back those who are stumbling to the slaughter. If you say, "Behold, we did not know this," does not he who weighs the heart perceive it? Does not he who keeps watch over your soul know it, and will he not requite man according to his work?

With a daily abortion rate of nearly 300 in our nation, the day of adversity is upon us. We will not fool God or escape his judgment if we pretend not to know this. Instead of pretence, instead of fainting, let us "be strong in the Lord and in the strength of his might" (Eph 6:10), doing all we can to rescue those who are being taken away to death.

In Defence of the Unborn

Induced abortion involves the deliberate destruction of an embryo or a foetus* in the womb through surgical or chemical means. How we view this practice will largely depend on whether or not we agree with the arguments put forward to justify it.

The beginning of life

People in favour of abortion argue that human life does not begin at conception. They maintain that the foetus is merely a *potential* human being. Supposedly, then, "nature" intervenes at some arbitrary point to confer humanity upon the foetus. Yet advocates of this view cannot explain when the foetus actually becomes a human being. Is it after the first trimester—that is, the first three months of growth? Is it when the foetus is viable—that is, able to survive outside the mother's womb? Is it upon birth after nine months gestation? They cannot say.

People opposed to abortion, however, maintain that human life begins at the beginning—that is, at conception. For it is both a biological and a logical fact that life commences when a sperm and an ovum unite. If this life is not "terminated", the foetus will grow into an infant, then into a child, then into an adolescent, and then into an adult.

If left alone, the foetus (Latin for "young one" or "offspring") will grow into a recognisable human being, never anything else. A woman does not become pregnant and then wonder what she will give birth to. She might wonder if the young one she carries will be normal or handicapped, healthy or sick, male or female, but she never wonders if her offspring will be human.

Stages of development

Advocates of abortion claim that the unborn child is merely "a blob of protoplasm" or a "mass of tissue". This is utterly untrue.

The baby's blood cells form as early as the seventeenth day. His (or her) eyes begin to form around the nineteenth day. His nervous system begins to form around the twentieth day. His heart begins regular pulsations (a legal sign of life) around the twenty-fifth day. His cerebral cortex begins to form around the thirty-third day, with brain waves being recordable ten days later.

Around seven weeks (before most abortions are performed) the unborn child is *recognisably* human, with a miniature head, face and body, and tiny arms, legs, fingers and toes. Around eight weeks all his organs—brain, liver, kidneys and stomach—are functioning. Around the tenth week he can squint, swallow, kick, and grasp.

If women were told these facts, they would not so easily succumb to the lie that life in the womb is merely a blob of protoplasm that can be destroyed at a whim.

Complete from conception

However, as important as these facts and this argument may be, there is a deeper fact and a stronger argument yet. The child is actually complete from conception. There is never a moment when another gene is added to determine his sex or eye-colour or some other characteristic. He is complete, needing only nutrition, oxygen and protection.

Consequently, it is not quite correct to say, for example, that the child's brain begins to form around the thirty-third day. The truth is, the blueprint is there from conception, contained in the chromosomes and genes.

Just as a woman cannot be a little bit pregnant, a foetus cannot be a little bit human. From conception, he is as fully human as his mother is fully pregnant. As has been said by others, the foetus is not a potential human being but a human being with great potential.

Viability outside the womb

Some people argue that it is all right to abort a child before he is viable—

that is, before he can live unaided outside the womb. Children born eighteen weeks prematurely (after only twenty-two weeks gestation) have been known to survive with adequate medical care. Until this point, however, they cannot survive outside the womb and are therefore, some argue, suitable candidates for abortion. This is a curious logic for two reasons.

Firstly, helplessness is not a justification for extermination. What has a child's frailty got to do with his right to life? A person is not expendable simply because he is vulnerable. In humane, civilised societies, the defenceless are viewed as candidates not for wanton destruction but for special protection. It is mischievous to attempt to validate abortion by arguments about the viability of the foetus. A child who is helpless has a special right to care and protection, and persons entrusted with such care and protection have a special obligation to deliver it.

Arguments about the viability of the foetus are illogical in a second way. If independence is a condition for survival, then a child who is born at term is not safe either. For even after nine months in the womb, a child is utterly dependent upon his mother. As far as dependency is concerned, a baby's situation before birth is exactly the same as his situation after birth. While the nature of the nutrition and care that a child requires may change, the need for it does not. Whether his nutrition comes via the umbilical cord or the breast, whether his shelter comes from the womb or the bunny rug—either way, a child is utterly helpless, utterly dependent. If inability to survive unaided is not a valid argument for infanticide, nor is it a valid argument for abortion.

A part of a woman's body

Some people claim that a foetus is a part of a woman's body, and therefore may be treated as she pleases. This is a mistaken assumption.

An unborn child is *not* a part of a woman's body, like an appendix or a tooth. He is an independent person, with his own brain, heart, organs and body. His genetic structure is different from his mother's and his blood may be of a different type. Indeed, if the baby *is* a *he*, even his sex is different! Both before and after birth, a child is an independent being who happens to be dependent on his mother for care and nutrition.

Abortion is not about a woman's right to control her own body. It is about her right to control—or more accurately, to destroy—another person's body, namely, her child's.

Right to choose

Proponents of abortion claim to be "pro-choice". Through this euphemism they imply that opponents of abortion are somehow opposed to women's rights. This simply is not true.

Those who support an unborn child's right to life also support a woman's right to choose in matters of sex, procreation and parenting. Every woman has a right to choose to marry or not to marry. She has a right to choose the times and circumstances for sexual intimacy with her husband. She has a right to choose to use or not to use non-abortive contraception. She has a right to choose to keep her child or (if she cannot cope) to offer him up for adoption. She has a right to receive full emotional and financial support from her child's father. But she does *not* have a "right" to choose to kill her child. No such "right" exists.

A woman's right to choose is limited by her child's right to life. The right to life underlies *every* other right, because without it a person cannot exercise *any* other right. No one enjoys the right to choose who does not first enjoy the right to life. Consequently, the right to life must take precedence over the right to choose. The right to choose is limited, but the right to life is absolute.

Right to life of the mother

Every human being has a right to life. This includes, of course, pregnant women. Consequently, on the exceptionally rare occasion when a woman is in mortal danger from the continuation of a pregnancy, her life cannot be forfeited against her will for the sake of the baby's. Where there is a genuine conflict between the right to life of the child and the right to life of the mother, it is legitimate to choose in favour of the mother.

However, "abortion" is hardly an appropriate term in such a tragic circumstance, for the intention is quite different. A doctor who induces labour and delivers the child of a woman who is about to die from toxaemia, for example, intends not to kill the child but to save the mother. And there is always the hope that the premature child, too, can be saved. If this hope proves vain, a death occurs, but not a murder.

Women's issue

Pro-abortionists often claim that abortion is a "women's issue" about which men have no right to speak. While it is true that abortion is of particular concern to women, it is not of exclusive concern to them. Men are also concerned about it for six reasons.

Firstly, all men were once unborn children. They therefore share a common heritage and humanity with the unborn. Having escaped abortion themselves, men have a legitimate concern to help others escape.

Secondly, half the children aborted are males. Even if they are denied the right to defend unborn girls, men cannot be denied the right to speak against the killing of unborn boys.

Thirdly, women do not get pregnant by themselves. Every child has a father, and fathers have a right to love and protect their sons and daughters.

Fourthly, the right to life is not a gender-specific issue. Men have just as much interest in the sanctity of human life as women.

Fifthly, men, no less than women, are moral beings capable of making moral judgments, even on matters outside their direct experience. Just as a person who is unaffected by ethnic cleansing in Rwanda or Bosnia can make a moral judgment about ethnic cleansing, so a person who is unaffected by abortion can make a moral judgment about abortion.

Sixthly, men, no less than women, are emotional beings capable of empathising with others. They can—and many *do*—feel distress at the plight of babies who face a gruesome death by abortion. Furthermore, they can—and many *do*—feel distress at the plight of women who suffer grief and guilt after having abortions. They have a right, therefore, to strive to save babies from death and mothers from guilt.

On a negative note, men have a right to speak against abortion because many of their own gender are implicated in the crime. Husbands and boyfriends often urge women to have abortions. Some even bully and blackmail women to do so. Good men have not just a right but an obligation to counter the actions of bad men.

Besides, pro-abortionists are hypocritical when they demand that men keep out of the abortion issue. What they really mean is that *pro-life* men must keep out. They don't at all mind male journalists writing pro-abortion articles or male politicians giving pro-abortion speeches or male judges giving pro-abortion rulings or male doctors performing abortions. They want to silence men (and women, for that matter) *who don't agree with them.*

Responsibility for unaborted babies

In another effort to muzzle debate, pro-abortionists claim that pro-lifers have no right to speak up for babies who face abortion unless they are personally prepared to raise those babies. This is nonsense.

Do individuals have to agree to rear abused children before they may speak against child abuse? Do they have to agree to house children with their legs blown off before they may speak against the use of land mines? No, and no again! Nor do they have to accept personal responsibility for unborn children before they may cry out against the aborting of those children!

The responsibility of raising a child lies squarely with the parents of that child. Hopefully, extended families, friends and community groups will help parents with this responsibility. Various government agencies may also be able to help. If parents feel quite unable to rear the child themselves, fostering and adoption are alternatives. But abortion is not.

Having said this, it should be noted that many pro-life individuals and agencies give significant practical and emotional support to women who experience crisis pregnancies. They do this not because justice demands it but because mercy desires it.

Health issue

Many people claim that abortion is a "health issue". This is quite untrue. Few of the 100,000 abortions performed annually in Australia are performed for health reasons. They are performed because men and women find it emotionally or socially or economically *inconvenient* to have a child.

I don't want a baby. I'm not ready to become a mother. My life will be disrupted. My career will be set back. My lifestyle will be ruined. Our relationship will suffer. These are the sorts of excuses women give for having abortions, and they clearly have no bearing on physical health.

In all bar the most exceptional cases, abortion has nothing to do with preserving good health—at least, so far as the mother is concerned. As far as the baby is concerned, it destroys good health. Abortion, it has been said, is the only operation known to mankind where two people go into the operating theatre and only one comes out.

Medical complications

In the context of health, it is worth noting that abortion is not always a routine, safe operation, as advocates of abortion would have women believe. Many complications can arise from the procedure.

Haemorrhaging, laceration to the cervix, perforation of the uterus, infection in the fallopian tubes and/or the ovaries: these are some of the well-documented short-term complications that can arise from abortion. Long term complications can include heavy menstrual bleeding, ectopic pregnancy, miscarriage, infertility, and a heightened risk of breast cancer.

Emotional complications

The possible medical complications are minor compared to the probable emotional complications arising from abortion. Guilt, depression and anger are experiences common to women who abort their babies.

The emotional and mental trauma suffered by many women after abortion is poignantly expressed by one young woman, Samantha, in a university student newspaper. Samantha, a first year arts student, reveals how as a teenager she became pregnant to a twenty-one year old man. He refused to marry her, and her mother urged her to have an abortion.

"My Mother had virtually convinced my Father that for me to have this baby would be the ruination of my life," Samantha writes. "In retrospect, me not having the baby was the ruination of my life ... I was 17, confused and severely emotionally traumatised. I passively accepted their solution."

Samantha continues: "We now reach the point of no return. The night my pregnancy was terminated. I know that for [my boyfriend] the horror of that night has left him and only remains as a distant memory. To an extent that is true of my Mother as well. However, for me, that night lives in my memory and dreams, causing distress almost regularly and it's now six years since the event."

In the same newspaper, another student wrote: "There is something really quite strange about actively seeking to have a new life scraped and vacuumed from your uterus ... I couldn't work for the first six months [after the abortion]. I couldn't know, from one hour to the next, whether I would be crying hysterically ... immobile in depression, or tentatively daring to function as a human being. I would sometimes be depressed for three weeks at a time, dressing and preparing meals was as much [as] I could do."[1]

Depression can be a precursor to suicide, and various studies have found that women who have had abortions are six-to-nine times more likely than other women to commit suicide.

Compassion

A charge sometimes levelled at opponents of abortion is that they are lacking in compassion. Lacking in compassion for whom? In truth, persons who oppose abortion are the only ones who show compassion for children in the womb.

However, the compassion of pro-lifers is not limited to unborn children. They are deeply concerned for the well-being of expectant mothers, too. They know that it is not compassionate to women to encourage them to have abortions by telling them that they are merely getting rid of "the products of conception". It is deeply cruel to deceive women into believing that the foetus is merely a mass of tissue and that abortion is merely a medical operation, thereby encouraging them to take a course of action that will in all probability lead to lifelong grief and guilt.

Unwanted children

Some people imply that abortion is an act of compassion towards the child, who might otherwise be abused by parents who do not want him. Apart from the fact that the prospect of abuse is pure supposition, it is a curious logic which says that in order to stop child abuse we must kill children. Abortion is itself the ultimate in child abuse.

Advocates of abortion maintain that society will be overwhelmed with unwanted children if abortion is not freely available. Their slogan is, "Every child a wanted child." Three things must be said in response to this.

Firstly, being unwanted is not a capital offence. Many people in our society are unwanted but this does not mean that they can be killed with impunity.

Secondly, the number of children who would ultimately be unwanted by their parents is grossly overestimated. Pregnancy catches many couples unawares; and consequently their first reaction may be one of anger or dismay. But given the very time that abortion denies, this reaction usually changes. Most children who are initially unwanted end up being deeply wanted and dearly loved.

Thirdly, even the small percentage of children who might be genuinely unwanted by their natural parents would not be altogether unwanted. There are thousands of couples who yearn to adopt children.

Backyard abortions

Pro-abortionists claim that women will die from backyard abortions if legal abortions are not freely available. This is untrue.

Firstly, since the advent of antibiotics, few women have died from abortions, whether legal or illegal. For example, according to the Australian Bureau of Statistics, in 1969 (before abortion was legal in any state, and before a single abortion clinic was in operation), only one woman died from an illegal abortion in the whole of Australia. The notion of women dying in droves from backyard abortions is a complete fabrication.

Secondly, laws against abortion actually protect women from backyard abortions. Where abortion is illegal, abortionists (whether backyard or front office) can be punished.

Thirdly, if abortions are not freely available, many women will not have them. Therefore they will not be exposed to danger.

Fourthly, no woman need die from a backyard abortion because no woman need have one. Backyard abortions do not become compulsory when legal abortions become unobtainable. They are performed only after women have deliberately and unlawfully sought them out.

Fifthly, while everyone laments the prospect of a woman suffering harm from a backyard abortion, such harm, should it occur, is not unjust. Abortion should not be legalised for fear that a few women may fall victim to their own schemes to kill their own babies.

Sixthly, it is monstrous to trade the actual deaths of 100,000 babies for the hypothetical deaths of a few women.

Besides all this, it is naive to think that legal abortions eliminate all dangers.

In her book *The Scarlet Lady*,[2] Carol Everett gives a harrowing account of the numerous "botched abortions" performed in the two clinics she managed for many years in the United States. One woman had her uterus perforated and her urinary tract severed by forceps. Another had her bowel pulled through a perforation in her uterus by the suction. Others died. These injuries occurred at the hands of qualified doctors in legal clinics.

Personal morality

Pro-abortionists claim that abortion is a matter of personal morality. There is an element of truth in this, but it is by no means the whole truth.

Abortion is not exclusively a personal issue because another person's life is at stake. It is not exclusively a personal issue because other people must be involved in providing the "service". It is not exclusively a personal issue because governments must legislate to facilitate it. It is not exclusively a personal issue because taxpayers are forced to subsidise it. It is not exclusively a personal issue because it reduces the nation's birth rate so that immigration must be increased to prevent an overall decline in population. It is not exclusively a personal issue because it affects how the whole community views and values human life.

The issue of abortion goes beyond personal morality to social justice. Indeed, it begins with *im*morality and ends with *in*justice!

Giving the facts

Abortion advocates insist that a woman contemplating abortion should not be confused by moral claims, but rather should be "given sufficient objective information to make her choice."

Two false assumptions about morality underlie this assertion. The first is that questions of morality can be divorced from questions of conduct. However, it is impossible to make choices concerning life and death without considering questions of good and evil, right and wrong. The second misconception is that morality is subjective rather than objective. However, right and wrong do not depend on internal preferences but on external standards.

Nonetheless, it is right that women contemplating abortion should be given objective information. Without doubt, they *should* be told the facts, which can be put simply as follows: Foetal science has unquestionably established what logic and faith knew all along—namely, that from conception the unborn child is a unique human being who, if left to live, will grow through the same stages of infancy, childhood, adolescence and adulthood as any other human being. Women cannot make informed decisions if facts about the foetus are concealed from them.

Prenatal facts always favour the unborn. Pro-lifers are not the ones who want to keep those facts from pregnant women.

Conclusion

Human life is immensely precious and ought to be afforded protection before and after birth. Abortion is an outrage against human life, and so should not be tolerated in any society that aspires to be compassionate and just. Such a society ought to act always in defence of the unborn.

---

* For convenience, I will use the term "foetus" to cover life in utero from conception to birth.

If People Were Dogs and Other False Arguments for Euthanasia

Enthusiasm for euthanasia is growing in Western societies. Enthusiasts argue: "People should have the choice to end their life if the quality of their life falls below some standard."[1] And again: "If people were dogs, we'd put them out of their misery." According to such arguments, we have a right to euthanasia because we are the sovereigns of death and the equals of animals. But are we? Before answering these and other pro-euthanasia arguments, it is worth clarifying the definition of euthanasia itself.

The meaning of euthanasia

The word *euthanasia* comes from two Greek words—*eu*, meaning, "good, well, easy"; and *thanatos*, meaning, "death". So euthanasia, which is sometimes called "mercy killing", means the administration of a good and easy death. It is the deliberate act of killing someone in order to end suffering. It entails consciously causing a person's death out of supposed compassion for that person. *Voluntary* euthanasia involves killing with the consent of the victim, while *involuntary* euthanasia involves killing without the victim's request or consent. Helping someone to kill himself (assisted suicide) is one aspect of voluntary euthanasia.

It is worth clarifying, however, that euthanasia has little to do with refusing futile or extreme medical treatment. The man who rejects a heart transplant or declines a second course of chemotherapy is not committing suicide, but rather is accepting the inevitability of his own death. The doctor who withholds or withdraws undue treatment at the request of a terminally ill patient is not killing his patient, but rather is refusing to prolong his patient's life at any cost.

Risks associated with palliative care are also quite unrelated to euthanasia. In rare instances, pain inhibiting drugs may inadvertently hasten the death of a patient. This is not euthanasia, for the aim in using the drugs is not to induce death but to alleviate suffering. Euthanasia always involves an intention to kill.

The right to refuse futile treatment and the right to receive adequate pain relief have no necessary connection with euthanasia. Properly understood, euthanasia involves (regardless of method) a deliberate and determined act to end a patient's life—nothing more and nothing less. The motive may be "mercy", but the objective is always "killing".

Personal choice

According its advocates, euthanasia is purely a personal affair. People should be free to choose to end their lives because such a choice is entirely individual and private.

On reflection, however, it is evident that euthanasia is not merely a personal matter. It is more than personal if it requires society to change its attitude to the sanctity of human life. It is more than personal if it encourages the community to view killing as a form of compassion and an alternative to care. It is more than personal if it requires governments to revise laws to allow certain types of homicide and suicide. It is more than personal if it requires doctors to assist in the killing. It is more than personal if it desensitises medical staff to the preciousness of human life. It is more than personal if it robs friends and relatives of extra time with a loved one. It is more than personal if it weakens a family's will to make sacrifices to care for one of its members. It is more than personal if it creates an atmosphere in which other weak or unwanted people feel pressured to choose to die.

The Problem of Confinement

Once the principle of mercy killing is accepted in law, it cannot be confined to those who give their consent. Voluntary and involuntary euthanasia go hand in hand. According to the Dutch government's *Remmelink Report*, for example, of the thousands of people who have their lives deliberately shortened or terminated by medical staff in Holland each year, over half are non-voluntary. "In the practice of euthanasia in the Netherlands," says Dr John Flemming,

Director of the Southern Cross Bioethics Institute in Adelaide, "more are killed without their knowledge and consent than with their knowledge and consent."[2]

Dr Karel Gunning, a medical practitioner in Rotterdam, Holland, cites an instance of involuntary euthanasia: "A friend of mine, an intern, was asked to see a lady with lung cancer, being very short of breath and having at most a fortnight to live. After the examination he asked the patient to come to the hospital for a few days. She refused, being afraid to be euthanised there. 'But I myself am on duty this weekend. Come on Saturday morning and I'll admit and help you.' So the lady came. On Sunday night she breathed normally and felt far better. The doctor went home and, being off duty on Monday morning, came back Monday afternoon. Then the patient was dead. The doctor's colleague had said: 'What is the sense of having that woman here. It makes no difference whether she dies today or after two weeks. We need that bed for another case.' So the lady was euthanised against her explicit wish."[3]

In addition to logic, research indicates that Australia would soon follow the Dutch example if voluntary euthanasia were legalised. A Flinders University survey of doctors and nurses in South Australia, for example, revealed that nineteen percent of doctors and nurses had taken active steps to bring about the death of a patient, despite the fact that euthanasia is illegal in that state. Forty-nine percent of these euthanasia-practising doctors said that they had never received a request from a patient to take such active steps.[4] If this happens when euthanasia of any sort is illegal, it is certain to happen all the more if euthanasia of some sort is legal.

Voluntary euthanasia inevitably gives rise to involuntary euthanasia. This in turn gives rise to distrust in doctors. Where euthanasia is sanctioned, the elderly and the seriously ill cannot be confident that medical staff will treat them rather than terminate them. To legalise euthanasia is to generate anxiety and distrust in the hearts of people at a time when they most need comfort and assurance.

Doctors are not the only danger when it comes to the practice of involuntary euthanasia. Relatives can be a threat, too. They can pressure a seriously ill person to "choose" euthanasia. This is already happening in Holland, where "In some cases, a patient's 'right to die' has subtly become a duty to die." Amsterdam psychiatrist Frank Koerselman observes, "I frequently see people pressured towards euthanasia by exhausted and impatient relatives." He cites an example of "a woman whose relatives gathered in Amsterdam for her planned euthanasia. One relative came from overseas. When the patient expressed last-minute doubts, the family said, 'You can't have her come all this way for nothing.' Instead of ensuring that the patient's true wishes were observed, the doctor carried out the euthanasia."[5]

Once it is socially acceptable and legally permissible, euthanasia cannot be confined to those who choose it. Nor can it be confined to those who are dying from incurable ailments. The practice soon widens from the terminally ill to the chronically ill and from the physically diseased to the mentally distressed. Again, in Holland, for example, euthanasia is applied to old people who "suffer" from loneliness. This fact was highlighted at a Death, Dying and Euthanasia Conference at the University of Queensland, where one conference speaker casually described a conversation with a Dutch doctor at a cocktail party in Holland.[6]

Endeavouring to justify her country's widespread practice of euthanasia through lethal injections, the Dutch doctor cited the case of a highly cultured woman in her eighties who "got lonelier and lonelier and lonelier" after her husband's death. "We used to visit her every week," the doctor said. "And every week she'd say to us, 'Please give me a lethal injection.' So after about three months we did."

The doctor concluded, "It was a terrible situation. She had nothing to live for. She had no family. Her friends had all died. Her husband who had been the centre of her life in every way was gone."

Interestingly, the conference speaker responded, "Did you think about buying her a cat?" To which the doctor replied seriously, "What a good idea!"

This sad, true story touches the heart of euthanasia: It requires no effort on the part of those who administer it. It was easier to end the woman's life than to end her loneliness. But with a little imagination (buy her a cat) and self-sacrifice (visit her more often), her loneliness could have been minimised and her life preserved.

For a selfish society, euthanasia is an easy solution—and that is what makes it such a horror.

Mixed motives

Advocates of euthanasia claim for themselves the noblest of motives—namely, compassion for those who are suffering. All they want, they say, is to receive or to administer a quick and painless death as a means to end suffering. No doubt this is a genuine motive for many.

However, the motives behind mercy killing are not always so noble. Some are very ugly indeed. One such motive is selfishness, as Dr Karel Gunning reveals in the following anecdote.

Commenting on how much morphine is needed to kill a patient, a Dutch colleague said to Dr Gunning, "I remember a case of an old man, who might die any day. Then this son came to see me and said: 'Doctor, my wife and I have booked a holiday, which we can't cancel. We don't want to come back for father's funeral, so please arrange that the burial is over before we leave.'" Obligingly, the doctor went along one morning and gave the old man a huge dose of morphine. Returning in the evening to pronounce the old man's death, the doctor was surprised to find him "sitting happily on the edge of his bed, having had an excellent day without pain." Dr Gunning concluded: "This colleague told the story as if it was the most normal thing to do, complying with the family's desire to have father buried before the holiday started."[7]

We should not blindly trust supporters of euthanasia just because they speak of "dignity" and "compassion". People often try to conceal their selfishness by professing a concern for others. Judas did this. When Mary of Bethany anointed the feet of Jesus with expensive perfume, he grumbled, "Why was this ointment not sold for three hundred denarii and given to the poor?" (John 12:5) On the face of it, this seems to be a reasonable sentiment. Granted, Judas may have been a little insensitive towards Jesus on this occasion, but his motive was noble. He was concerned for the poor. Or was he? The apostle John discloses that Judas spoke in these pious terms not because he cared for the poor but because he was a thief, and used to steal the money entrusted to him by Jesus and the other disciples. Advocates of euthanasia do not always mean what they say when they speak of respect for human dignity and compassion for the suffering. Their motives are often suspect.

The Lord Jesus taught his disciples to pray to the Father, "lead us not into temptation—do not put us to the test" (Matt 6:13). Why is this? In part it is because we are morally weak and liable to succumb to temptation. Laws that permit euthanasia put people to the test. They tempt people to act selfishly. They open the possibility for relatives to hasten death to avoid inconvenience. They open the possibility for children to hasten death to gain their inheritance. They open the possibility for doctors to hasten death to free up hospital beds. They open the possibility for governments to hasten death to avoid the costs of medical care. In short, laws permitting euthanasia open possibilities that should not be opened. In doing so, they lead us into temptation.

Treating humans like animals

Just as noble talk can conceal base motives, so a clever question can confuse sound sentiments. One such question often posed by the advocates of euthanasia is: "We put animals out of their misery, so why not humans?" This question insinuates that the opponents of euthanasia are callous and uncaring. It implies that they are prepared to treat animals better than humans. It cleverly links mercy with death and misery with life, so that to argue for life is to argue for misery.

From a Christian point of view, however, the answer to this question is simple: We don't put humans out of their misery as we do animals because humans are not animals.

While human beings are similar to animals on a biological level, they are utterly dissimilar on a spiritual level. Unlike animals, humans posses conscience, imagination, reason, personality, a longing for purpose, and an impulse to worship. These are spiritual qualities that lift us from the animal kingdom into a kingdom all our own.

The extraordinary difference between humans and animals arises from the fact that humans bear the image of God. It is the spiritual likeness of God within us that makes us distinct and gives us our value.

All creatures are precious in God's sight. This is only to be expected, given that God made them all. But human beings are more precious to God than other creatures. This, too, is only to be expected, given that God made us like himself.

"Of how much more value is a man than a sheep!" Jesus exclaimed on one occasion (Matt 12:12). In saying this, he was not so much inviting a comparison as affirming an absolute: A human's life is valuable—much more valuable, in fact, than an animal's. Just how much more is unanswerable because it is immeasurable.

Yet, in a sense, a measure of a person's worth can be found in the Bible. That measure arises from two things.

The first is the Lord Jesus Christ himself. He is the measure of the value of every human life. He set aside his divine glory to come to earth from heaven to die for us. He did this to make amends to God the Father for our sins, so that all who trust in him may be forgiven and renewed forever. When contemplating the worth of human life, the implications of Christ's sacrifice are truly staggering. If God's Son laid down his life for us, then in some mysterious, thrilling, humbling way, the value of our lives is linked with the value of his life!

The second measure of the value of human life lies in the love of God. The astonishing message of the Bible is that God loves us. His love is evident from the fact that he sustains and blesses us. But the pre-eminent proof of his love is found in his willingness to sacrifice his Son to save us. Indeed, the Bible declares that "God demonstrates his own love for us in this: While we were still sinners, Christ died for us" (Rom 5:8; NIV). The cross is the demonstration of God's love; and his love is the estimation of our worth.

In short, by two immeasurable things—the life of Christ and the love of God—scripture provides a measure of the preciousness of human life. We simply cannot put a human out of his misery as we would a dog because all humans bear the image of God. This image is sacred, and must be respected and protected, as the life of Christ and the love of God confirm.

So to the suffering person who says, "If I was a dog, you'd shoot me," we should respond: "Yes, but you're not a dog. You're a human being, which makes you vastly more valuable. So rather than shoot you, we'll soothe you. Rather than end your life, we'll end your pain. We'll do all we can to heal you; and where that's not possible, we'll do all we can to comfort you; but we'll do nothing at all to kill you."

Death is not the end

Those who argue that humans should be put out of their misery like animals fail to appreciate that humans are superior to animals in both nature and worth.

They also fail to appreciate that misery does not necessarily end at death.

The Bible teaches that human beings are eternal beings. Although death marks the end of this life, it also marks the start of the next life. It is the doorway into eternity.

However, all people will not spend eternity in the same place. Some will go to heaven, while others will go to hell. Jesus taught that on the Day of Judgment he will separate the faithful from the unfaithful. To the faithful he will say, "Come, O blessed of my Father, inherit the kingdom prepared for you". To the unfaithful he will say, "Depart from me, you cursed, into the eternal fire prepared for the devil and his angels". Hence, the unrighteous "will go away into eternal punishment, but the righteous into eternal life" (Matt 25:34, 41, 46).

People who die without having their sins forgiven are not relieved of their suffering. On the contrary, they experience even greater suffering. They enter into a place of torment where, Jesus says, they will forever "weep and gnash their teeth" (Matt 8:12).

To hasten the death of someone in the hope of putting him out of his misery may well be a tragic mistake. For death is not the end of suffering— unless the sufferer is a Christian.

Only those whose sins are forgiven through faith in Jesus will enjoy happiness and well-being in eternity. This is a compelling reason to prolong, not shorten, life. For while a person is alive, there is yet hope that he will repent and believe and be saved.

The wonderful story of the penitent thief (Luke 23:39-43) illustrates the danger of shortening an unbeliever's life even by a few hours. This man was crucified with the Lord Jesus; and in the course of his agonising death, he asked Jesus for salvation. But imagine how different things would have been for him if some compassionate soul had offered him euthanasia before his crucifixion. "Look," this well-meaning person might have said, "the situation is hopeless. The Romans are going to crucify you tomorrow for sure. They are going to hammer nails through your hands and feet and hoist you up on a cross. You will probably hang there for one or two days before you die. The pain will be unbearable. But there's no need to suffer like that because I've smuggled a drug past the guards. If you just drink it, then you'll escape the agony, not to mention the indignity, of crucifixion. Come on, drink up! Under the circumstances, it's better to die today than tomorrow." On the surface, this well-intentioned person would have offered a merciful solution to the thief's predicament. But in reality, he would have caused the thief eternal misery. For it was only because of his suffering that the thief confessed his sin and called out to Jesus; and it was in response to his confession and call that Jesus said, "Today you will be with me in Paradise."

Death is not the end of existence, nor is it necessarily the end of suffering. Indeed, a person who is put out of his misery in this life may well be plunged into misery in the next life. Mindful of the wrath to come, we dare not hasten a person's death.

Acceptance of death

By way of counterbalance, however, it should be said that people who resist euthanasia do not always have to resist their own deaths. God has appointed a time for us to die (Heb 9:27), and Christians in particular should be prepared to accept his appointment. We should not try to cling frantically to life like those who have no hope. Such behaviour arises from fear, not faith, and loses sight of the fact that the Lord Jesus has conquered death on behalf of those who love him.

Opposition to euthanasia does not even mean that we must always desire life. There are times when it is natural and moral to welcome death. On one occasion the apostle Paul declared, "My desire is to depart and be with Christ, for that is far better" (Phil 1:23). Whether from weariness or suffering or homesickness, we may well reach a time when "we would rather be away from the body and at home with the Lord" (2 Cor 5:8). And although we are forbidden to take our own lives, we are nonetheless permitted to pray with Simeon, "Lord, now let your servant depart in peace" (Luke 2:29).

Suffering need not be futile

Thanks to advances in palliative care, few people in the Western world need suffer extreme physical pain during the final stages of terminal illness. Even so, there may well be suffering arising from a fear of death, an anxiety for loved ones, a loss of dignity, a loss of independence, and a deterioration in quality of life.

While no one welcomes such distress, Christians should recognise it as part of God's dealings with mankind. God uses suffering to wean us from sin and to win us to himself. He also uses it to develop endurance, character and hope in his people (Rom 5:3-4). Whether or not we can see it ourselves, God has a purpose in suffering. Instead of rebelling against him when we suffer, we should rely on him to help us through it and be responsive to him to learn from it.

Suffering is inevitable. But for God's people, it is not futile. Nor is it permanent. A time is coming when God will wipe every tear from our eyes. Indeed, "the sufferings of this present time are not worth comparing with the glory that is to be revealed to us" (Rom 8:18; cf 2 Cor 4:16-17). If we remember this, we will neither lose heart during suffering nor kill ourselves or others to end it.

The right to a good death

Advocates of euthanasia claim that "everyone has the right to a good death." Consequently, "we all have the right to make choices about what we will or won't find an acceptable way to live. And so we all have the right to choose what we will do when the quality of our lives becomes unacceptable." It is entirely up to us to decide whether we think this or that is "a good enough reason to die", and it is our prerogative to choose "how and when to die." Therefore we should have "full control" over our death so that we can be guaranteed of "dying with dignity".[8] Such claims are seriously mistaken.

Talk about the right to exercise full control over our death is simply bravado and bluster. No one has a "right" to anything so far as death is concerned. None of us knows how or when we will die, and none of us can add a single hour to our lives (Matt 6:22). Our ignorance and impotence are absolute. Euthanasia is not a means of gaining control over death but of capitulating to it.

Furthermore, talk about the right to determine the time and method of our death is arrogance and rebellion. It is an affront to the sovereignty of God. He alone is the giver, sustainer, owner and terminator of all life. Consequently, he alone has the right to choose how and when we will die. "All souls are mine," the Lord declares (Ezek 18:4). They are created when he sends forth his Spirit; and they die when he takes away their breath (Ps 104:29-30). "So then, whether we live or whether we die, we are the Lord's" (Rom 14:8). We cannot do what we please with our lives because our lives do not belong solely to us. We hold them in trust.

Talk about the right to die if conditions becomes personally unacceptable limits the value of life to the quality of life. However, unlike the quality of life, the value of life does not vary with circumstances. It is not arbitrary but absolute. Human life is to be valued in every circumstance. We are not at liberty to kill ourselves or others when things are not to our liking. We do not have an absolute right to determine what we will and will not put up with. Rather, like the apostle Paul we have a responsibility to learn, in whatever state we are, to be content. We must learn "the secret of facing plenty and hunger, abundance and want." That secret is found in the realisation that we can do all things through Christ who strengthens us (Phil 4:11-13).

Talk about "a good death" and "death with dignity" is also misguided. The process of death may be "good" in the negative sense that it is quick rather than slow or painless rather than painful. But it can never be good in a positive sense. Physically at least, there are no benefits in the dying process. And death itself is anything but good. It is a horror and an outrage. It entered human experience because of sin (Rom 5:12) and is a chief means by which Satan has subjected us to fear and bondage (Heb 2:14). It is "the last enemy to be destroyed" (1 Cor 15:26). There is no goodness or dignity in it. On the contrary, death is the ultimate indignity, the ultimate degradation, of human life.

From a Christian point of view, what constitutes a good death is not the absence of pain but the presence of faith. It is through faith in God that we receive divine approval (Heb 11:2). However, such approval may actually contribute to our suffering in this life. The Bible records how some of the faithful who enjoyed God's approval "were tortured, refusing to accept release, that they might rise again to a better life. Others suffered mocking and scourging, and even chains and imprisonment. They were stoned, they were sawn in two, they were killed with the sword ..." (Heb 11:35-37). There was nothing dignified about the deaths of these believers. Nonetheless, their deaths were good in the only sense that matters: they died for and with God.

Conclusion

Naturally, we should avoid suffering where possible; but we should not avoid it at any cost. For while freedom from suffering is desirable, it is not the highest good.

Writing from a Roman prison, Paul said his desire was that "with full courage now as always Christ will be honoured in my body, whether by life or by death" (Phil 1:20). This should be the principal goal of all God's people. To that end, in the face of mounting enthusiasm for euthanasia, we would be wise to pray, "Father, lead us not into temptation, but deliver us from evil."

Mistaken Support for Euthanasia

While listening to a radio talkback show, I was moved by the sad stories of two men who called to express their support for euthanasia, or mercy killing.

The first man related how his elderly mother had suffered during the final stages of cancer. On one occasion, he asked a nurse to do something to relieve his mother's pain, only to be told that his mother was not due for her next morphine injection for another half-hour. He became angry and insisted that she be given a painkiller immediately. After this confrontation, he consulted with the doctors about the management of his mother's pain. They were reluctant to administer additional morphine for fear of shortening her life. But eventually they agreed to allow larger and more frequent doses. After this, his mother lived several more months, largely free from pain.

The second man recounted how his twenty-year-old daughter had contracted a fatal brain tumour. Chemotherapy did more harm than good and she lapsed into a coma. The medication she was given while in the coma bloated her body. The pressure from the tumour forced one of her eyes from its socket. But the doctors kept her alive by keeping her hooked up to various life support systems, including an artificial respirator. The man begged the doctors to disconnect the respirator, but they refused. As his daughter's condition became more grotesque, he became more enraged. When the doctors eventually agreed to turn off the respirator, the young woman died within minutes.

Who could remain unmoved by the heart-rending stories of these two men? Who could deny the correctness of their requests concerning their loved ones? Surely, what they endured was wrong and what they wanted was right!

But do these men's stories illustrate the need for euthanasia? Contrary to the opinions of the men themselves, they do not. Rather, they illustrate a widespread misunderstanding about what euthanasia really is.

Euthanasia involves premeditated killing—deliberate killing—for supposed compassionate reasons. In its most usual form, it involves injecting chemicals into a person's veins in order to kill him or her.

If the men who phoned the talkback show had been clear on this, they would not have expressed support for euthanasia. For neither one had requested a lethal injection for his loved one.

The son did not ask the doctors to kill his elderly mother. He asked them to end her pain. He accepted the risk that her life might be shortened as a result, but he considered it a risk worth taking. Neither he nor the doctors had any intention of killing his mother by increasing her dosage of morphine. Their sole intention was to make her comfortable during the last days of her life. So then, what this man wanted was not euthanasia but adequate pain relief. He wanted appropriate palliative care.

As for the father, he did not ask the doctors to kill his daughter. He asked them to disconnect her life-support equipment. He accepted the inevitability of her death, and was not prepared to allow her life to be prolonged indefinitely by artificial means. He knew the time had come to let go. He asked the doctors to stop playing God and to allow "nature" to take its course. So then, what he wanted was not euthanasia but an end to useless, degrading treatment.

Euthanasia involves purposely killing a person by lethal injection. It should not be confused with the use of painkillers that may inadvertently shorten a patient's life. The unintentional hastening of death cannot be equated with the intentional taking of life.

Furthermore, euthanasia should not be confused with the discontinuation of treatment. A decision to shorten life is quite different from a decision not to prolong life. The injection of a lethal chemical is not the same as the withdrawal of a futile treatment.

It is true that there are grey areas so far as the discontinuation of treatment is concerned. Some decisions may be difficult and open to question. But there are no grey areas, no uncertainties, so far as euthanasia is concerned. It is the deliberate dealing out of death and it is uniformly black.

The experiences of the two men on talkback radio do *not* support euthanasia. But they *do* support the need for better palliative care and a reappraisal of the notion that life must be prolonged at any cost.

From a Christian perspective, to care for the dying is a noble thing, and to accept their death is a necessary thing, but to induce their death is an evil thing.

Human beings are incalculably precious because God created us in his image for eternal companionship with himself. When we turned away from him, he demonstrated his love for us by sending his Son to turn us back. In this way, he invested us with immeasurable value, and for this reason we must hold ourselves and each other to be sacred.

One way to uphold the sanctity of human life is to spell out exactly what euthanasia is and is not. For a mistaken understanding of euthanasia gives rise to a mistaken support for euthanasia. When we clear up the misunderstandings, we dry up the support.

A Biblical Perspective on Prostitution

Prostitution involves the selling and buying of sex. It involves an exchange of money for sex between a man and a woman* who have no legal, moral or emotional attachment to each other.

How should Christians view such activity? Fortunately, as with any matter of importance, God guides us to a right perspective through his written word.

The Bible teaches that sex is a good gift from God to any heterosexual couple who in love and law promise enduring and exclusive fidelity to one another. Sex is God's gift to every bride and groom, to be unwrapped on the honeymoon and enjoyed throughout the marriage. In short, scripture highly approves of sexual intimacy between a man and a woman for the purposes of pleasure, love and procreation, provided they have committed themselves to one another in the covenant of marriage.

When we appreciate what the Bible approves concerning sex, we can anticipate what it disapproves. Take prostitution. If scripture teaches that the only right context for sexual intimacy is marriage, then we can deduce that prostitution is wrong because it involves sexual intimacy outside that right context. And if scripture teaches that one of the good purposes for sexual intercourse is the expression of love, then we know implicitly that prostitution is bad because it deliberately severs the sexual act from that good purpose. So even if the Bible never specifically mentioned prostitution, we would know that it is wrong because it falls outside of what God commends as good in sexual matters.

However, the Bible does not merely imply that prostitution is wrong. It openly condemns the practice.

Being a prostitute is forbidden

The Bible warns against women engaging in prostitution. Leviticus 19:29 states, "Do not degrade your daughter by making her a prostitute". Prostitution degrades women. Consequently, a woman is not permitted to become a prostitute, and no one is permitted to make her one.

So serious is the degradation involved in prostitution, that Leviticus 21:9 declares, "If a priest's daughter defiles herself by becoming a prostitute, she disgraces her father; she must be burned in the fire." Through prostitution a woman stains herself and shames her relatives. Such evil is repulsive to God, and deserves severe punishment.

Note the reference to "daughter" in the two Leviticus texts. This reminds us that every prostitute is someone's daughter. She is not an object with sexual attributes but a person with family relationships. She is dear to the heart of some father and mother. Her welfare is their desire and her woe is their distress. The man who uses a prostitute is degrading not only a "woman" but also a "daughter".

Such is the vileness of prostitution that the Lord refuses to accept any money associated with it: "You must not bring the earnings of a female prostitute or of a male prostitute into the house of the LORD your God to pay any vow, because the LORD your God detests them both" (Deut 23:18). (Perhaps our governments could take a lesson from this. Instead of devising schemes to tax the illegal earnings of prostitutes, they should implement and enforce laws to put a stop to such earnings altogether.)

Throughout the Bible, prostitution is used as a symbol of filthiness and unfaithfulness, and God likens his people to prostitutes whenever they turn from him to false gods and to evil ways. In Ezekiel 23, for example, the Lord likens Jerusalem and Samaria to prostitutes because of their sin. "They became prostitutes in Egypt," the Lord declares, "engaging in prostitution from their youth. In that land their breasts were fondled and their virgin bosoms caressed" (v.3). As for Samaria, the Lord declares, she "engaged in prostitution while she was still mine; and she lusted after her lovers, the Assyrians … She gave herself as a prostitute to all the elite of the Assyrians and defiled herself with all the idols of everyone she lusted after" (vv.3, 5, 7). As for Jerusalem, the Lord declares, "in her lust and prostitution she was more depraved than her sister

[Samaria]. She too lusted after the Assyrians ... Then the Babylonians came to her, to the bed of love, and in their lust they defiled her. ... When she carried on her prostitution openly and exposed her nakedness, I turned away from her in disgust" (vv. 11-12, 17-18). Prostitution involves lust, depravity and defilement. It disgusts God, who uses it as an image for all that is disgusting.

Using a prostitute is forbidden

In addition to warning women not to become prostitutes, the Bible warns men not to use them.

Having told his fellow believers that their "bodies are members of Christ himself", the apostle Paul asks, "Shall I then take the members of Christ and unite them with a prostitute?" Although the answer is self-evident, Paul nonetheless replies emphatically, "Never!" (1 Cor 6:15). It is unthinkable that a man joined by love to Christ could be joined by lust to a prostitute.

Paul's insistence that men should shun prostitution is not confined to Christian men. He takes it for granted that it is impermissible and despicable for any man to have sex with a prostitute. His point is, however, that such an act is doubly inexcusable for Christian men. What is bad for a man without Christ is worse for a man with Christ.

Solomon also warns men to keep away from "the immoral woman". He declares: "Do not lust in your heart after her beauty or let her captivate you with her eyes, for the prostitute reduces you to a loaf of bread, and the adulteress preys upon your very life. Can a man scoop fire into his lap without his clothes being burned? Can a man walk on hot coals without his feet being scorched?" (Prov 6:24-28).

It is interesting to note that Solomon places the prostitute, not the man, in the position of power. She can lure him with her beauty and captivate him with her eyes. Speaking with the full support of the Holy Spirit, Solomon expresses a wisdom that is all but lost today. He points out that the physical beauty and sensual behaviour of women has extraordinary power over men. And prostitutes use that power to manipulate men for financial gain.

Of course, that men are weak in matters of sex in no way excuses them for succumbing to sexual immorality. Scripture advises several practical ways in which men can and should protect themselves from the power of a prostitute.

146

They should not dwell on her beauty in their hearts (Prov 6:24). They should "Keep to a path far from her" (Prov 5:8). They should seek sexual satisfaction with their own wives (Prov 5:15-20). A man who beds a prostitute is a man who snubs God's advice. He enters into his sordid liaison because he has given himself over to lust. His guilt is absolute.

Prostitutes are predators

But so, too, is the guilt of the prostitute. Scripture is ruthless in its denunciation of her, and equally ruthless in its reversal of the way we tend to look at her. It does not present her as a victim but as a victimiser. "Many are the victims she has brought down" (Prov 7:26).

The Bible portrays the prostitute as a predator. Solomon offers a vivid picture of how she preys on men in Proverbs 7:7-22:

> I saw among the simple, I noticed among the young men, a youth who lacked judgment. He was going down the street near her corner, walking along in the direction of her house ... Then out came a woman to meet him, dressed like a prostitute and with crafty intent. (She is loud and defiant, her feet never stay at home; now in the street, now in the squares, at every corner she lurks.) She took hold of him and kissed him and with a brazen face she said: "... I have perfumed my bed with myrrh, aloes and cinnamon. Come, let's drink deep of love till morning; let's enjoy ourselves with love! ..." With persuasive words she led him astray; she seduced him with her smooth talk. All at once he followed her like an ox going to the slaughter, like a deer stepping into a noose ...

Some men lust for prostitutes and go out of their way to find them. But not all. The young man Solomon describes was not intent on using a prostitute. He lacked judgment, not virtue. He was simply naïve. He innocently, if foolishly, walked down the street near the prostitute's corner. She did the rest. She was on the look out for him. She was lurking in wait for him. When he happened by, she pounced on him. She solicited him with smooth talk, seductive dress, provocative gestures and crafty intent. Then, although he had no prior intention to do so, *all at once* he followed her.

The active way a prostitute solicits the unwary is portrayed again in Proverbs 9:14-17: "She sits at the door of her house, on a seat at the highest point of the city, calling out to those who pass by, who go straight on their way. 'Let all who are simple come in here!' she says to those who lack judgment. 'Stolen water is sweet; food eaten in secret is delicious!'" The prostitute calls out to those who are going *straight on their way*. She is not passively waiting to receive those who actively seek her, nor is she on the lookout only for seedy characters who loiter about her door. She considers every man fair game. She tries to entice all who pass by. The decent husband, the naive youth—these are her marks every bit as much as the lecher and the drunkard. And why not? After all, her love is not for the men, but for their money.

Scripture declares that "the love of money is a root of all kinds of evil" (1 Tim 6:10). Certainly, on the female side, the love of money is the root of prostitution. The prostitute's primary motive is greed. She wants easy money, big money, the type of money that cannot be earned by proper means. "Every prostitute receives a fee" (Ezek 16:33). That is why she does it: that is her motive. And that is why she is such a predator: the more men she has, the more money she gets.

A glance at the personal columns in any major newspaper reveals just how predatory prostitutes are. Less explicit advertisements read: "Feel so good with me! Slim young pretty thing!"; "I'm 18, busty, size 10, attractive, just started, please teach me"; "Hot Aussie girl for your pleasure"; and "Slim, busty and very exotic oriental to fulfill your hidden desires".[1] Through the newspapers, prostitutes enter millions of homes every day to solicit other women's husbands, boyfriends, sons, brothers and fathers. That they succeed in enticing many of these men is evident from the fact that they keep on paying to place their advertisements week after week after week.

The Bible does not subscribe to the view that prostitutes are victims— victims of sad upbringings or difficult circumstances or men's lust. In some instances, of course, they may indeed be victims of these things. But that is not true for all. And it is not an excuse for any. Neither past misery nor present poverty nor masculine lechery excuses the prostitute for her greed and debauchery. Nor does it make amends for the damage she does.

Prostitutes cause harm

And the Bible insists that prostitution causes considerable damage indeed. It utterly rejects the notion that prostitution is a victimless crime, a harmless vice between consenting adults.

According to God's word, prostitution causes poverty. "A companion of prostitutes," Solomon warns, "squanders his wealth" (Prov 29:3). True to one of her names, a hooker gets a man hooked on her charms, then charges him exorbitantly for them. A former prostitute and madam has observed that "Some men steal TVs, they steal their wives' jewellery, in order to hock it to see a working girl. Some men spend a fortune on working girls. You always think: Are their families being fed?"[2] No wonder scripture warns, "the prostitute reduces you to a loaf of bread" (Prov 6:26).

Scripture indicates that prostitution also causes disloyalty and unfaithfulness. Solomon declares that "a prostitute is a deep pit ... Like a bandit she lies in wait, and multiplies the unfaithful among men" (Prov 23:27-28). As virtually all men are either husbands or future-husbands, the man who uses a prostitute is unfaithful either to his wife or to his future-wife. And as all men are commanded by God to avoid pre-marital sex (fornication) and extra-marital sex (adultery), the man who uses a prostitute is unfaithful to God's standards and therefore to God himself. And note that the prostitute *multiplies* the unfaithful among men. More men are unfaithful to their wives and to their Creator than would otherwise be the case were it not for the prostitute plying her trade.

The apostle Paul offers profound insight into the damage caused by prostitution (and all sexual immorality) in 1 Corinthians 6:13-20:

> The body is not meant for sexual immorality, but for the Lord, and the Lord for the body. By his power God raised the Lord from the dead, and he will raise us also. Do you not know that your bodies are members of Christ himself? Shall I then take the members of Christ and unite them with a prostitute? Never! Do you not know that he who unites himself with a prostitute is one with her in body? For it is said, "The two will become one flesh." But he who unites himself with the Lord is one with him in spirit. Flee from sexual immorality. All other sins a man commits are outside his body, but he who sins sexually sins

against his own body. Do you not know that your body is a temple of the Holy Spirit, who is in you, whom you have received from God? You are not your own; you were bought at a price. Therefore honour God with your body.

Paul's warning against prostitution centres on his understanding of the purpose and importance of the human body. His main points are: Our bodies are not meant to be used for illicit sexual pleasures (v.13). Our bodies are meant to be used as instruments for serving God (v.13). Our bodies are not extraneous to our being, but will be resurrected, restored and glorified on the Last Day (v.14). As Christians, as people who are "in Christ", our bodies are mysteriously and intimately connected with Christ (v.15). Being closely united with the Lord Jesus Christ, our bodies should not be closely united with prostitutes (v.15). Our bodies are integrated with our souls, so that sexual union is more than a physical union, and forms a bonding of emotions and affections (v.16). Our bodies are meant to become "one flesh" with only one other in marriage (v.16). Our bodies themselves are injured and disgraced by sexual sin in a unique way (v.18). Our bodies are the sanctified dwelling places of God's Spirit (v.19). Our bodies are not our sole property, but are owned by God (v.19). Our bodies (not just our souls) were bought by God for the ransom price of his Son's death (v.20). In the light of all this, our bodies should be given over to the glory of God (v.20).

From Paul's teaching it is evident that prostitution causes harm in a number of ways. It harms the intentions and standards of God concerning the proper use of the body. It harms the bodies (not to mention the personalities) of the prostitute and the prostitute-user. It harms the institution of marriage in principle and in practice. If the practitioners are Christians, it harms their relationship with the Lord Jesus who is united with them. It harms their relationship with the Holy Spirit who indwells them. It harms their relationship with the Father who ransomed them and owns them.

Or to put it another way, prostitution dishonours the purposes God ordained for the body. It dishonours the body itself. It dishonours marriage. And it dishonours the triune God in his relationship with us as Father, Son and Holy Spirit.

The ultimate damage that prostitution causes is death. The man who succumbs to the lure of a prostitute, Solomon says, is "like a bird darting into a snare, little knowing it will cost him his life." Solomon continues, "her slain are a mighty throng. Her house is a highway to the grave, leading down to the chambers of death" (Prov 7:23, 26-27). Solomon may be speaking of physical death, for certainly prostitution can involve such life-threatening things as disease, drugs, jealousy, depression and corruption. However, he is surely also speaking of spiritual death, that state of alienation from God which, if unchecked in this life, leads to damnation in the next life. Solomon seems to have spiritual death in mind again in Proverbs 9:18, where he says of men who are enticed into the prostitute's house, "little do they know that the dead are there, that her guests are in the depths of the grave." Men in a brothel may be alive physically, but they are spiritual zombies. Alive to lust, they are dead to love, dead to relationship, dead to fidelity, dead to purity, dead to reality. And all this death is both a cause and an effect of the ultimate death: death to God. Like the prostitute herself, the prostitute-user is dead to God, having no more communion with him than a corpse with a loved one. Truly, the dead, the damned, are there in the prostitute's house.

Prostitution leads to perdition. We should not dismiss or diminish this dreadful fact. "Do not be deceived," Paul says, "the sexually immoral ... will not inherit the kingdom of God" (1 Cor 6:9-10). As one form of sexual immorality, prostitution severs the prostitute and the prostitute-user from God and his kingdom. It produces death.

Prostitutes can be pardoned

People who engage in prostitution are dead in their sins and in danger of damnation. But God, being infinite in mercy and compassion, wants to remedy that. Although he threatens punishment, he offers pardon. Forgiveness and cleansing can be had for the asking.

The Bible contains two moving accounts of prostitutes who received forgiveness and cleansing. The first concerns a woman named Rahab. The second concerns a woman who is not named.

Rahab lived in Jericho over a thousand years before the birth of Jesus. She sheltered two Israelite men who had come to spy out the city. She did this because she had come to believe that "the LORD [their] God is God in heaven above and on the earth below" (Josh 2:11). So she turned from her false gods to the true and living God. She put her faith in him, and demonstrated the genuineness of her faith by what she did. As a consequence, God accepted her, and saved her from the calamity that came upon her people. He gave her a home among his people, the people of Israel. Rahab went on to marry one of the men of Israel, and her son became one of the ancestors of the Lord Jesus Christ. She is mentioned by Matthew (1:5) in the genealogy of Jesus. She is honoured in Hebrews (11:31) as one of the heroes of the faith. She is cited by James (2:25) as an example of how faith and action should exist together. Rahab stands as a lasting example of the forgiveness and restoration that God offers to the prostitute.

The second example of God's grace to prostitutes concerns an unnamed woman in Luke 7:36-50. This woman, whom Luke describes as "a woman who had lived a sinful life", was grieved by a sense of her own filthiness and gripped by a conviction that Jesus could cleanse her. On learning that Jesus was a guest at a particular house in her town, "she brought an alabaster jar of perfume, and as she stood behind him at his feet weeping, she began to wet his feet with her tears. Then she wiped them with her hair, kissed them and poured perfume on them." In response, Jesus said to her, "Your sins are forgiven. ... Your faith has saved you; go in peace."

Jesus was moved by this prostitute's brokenness and faith. He accepted her worship knowing full-well what she was. He did not pretend that she was basically a nice person, nor did he make excuses for her sin. He frankly acknowledged that she had much to be forgiven—and he freely forgave it! More than this, as his discussion with his self-righteous host reveals (vv.39-47), he indicated that the magnitude of her sin was outmatched by the magnitude of God's grace (cf Rom 5:20). And as if that were not enough, he further indicated that the enormity of her sin would work in her a correspondingly enormous love for God as she came to realise just how much she had been forgiven.

The wonder of it! Almighty God does not merely triumph over sin—he turns it to his advantage, using it to manifest his grace and thereby to multiply his people's love. How much they will love him, the prostitutes, if only they will get a sense of the horror of their sin and the splendour of God's grace!

Prostitute-users can be pardoned

Forgiveness, restoration and honour—this is what God in Christ offers to the prostitute, provided she turns from her sin and trusts in his Son. And the offer is not to the prostitute only. It is to the prostitute-user as well. Jesus illustrates this in his moving parable of the prodigal son in Luke 15:11-32.

There was a young man, Jesus said, who took his share of his father's property, then immediately "squandered [that] property with prostitutes" (vv.13, 30). The prostitutes, the profligate living, quickly reduced him to poverty, and he took a job feeding pigs. As he tended these symbols of his moral depravity, the young man came to his senses and decided to return home to cast himself on his father's mercy. So with shame and trepidation "he got up and went to his father. But while he was still a long way off, his father saw him and was filled with compassion for him; he ran to his son, threw his arms around him and kissed him. The son said to him, 'Father, I have sinned against heaven and against you. I am no longer worthy to be called your son.' But the father said to his servants, 'Quick! Bring the best robe and put it on him. Put a ring on his finger and sandals on his feet. Bring the fattened calf and kill it. Let's have a feast and celebrate. For this son of mine was dead and is alive again; he was lost and is found.' So they began to celebrate" (vv.20-24).

Oh, the grace of God! A man can squander his living on prostitutes and yet not be utterly without hope. God will forgive him yet, if only he will come to his senses. If only he will leave the pigsty of his sins, God will receive and restore him. And if he has no strength to leave, let him call out where he stands, and God will lift him out, lift him out with love and weeping. Let only a man cry out to God—"Father, I have sinned against heaven and against you. I am not worthy to be called your son. Forgive me!"—and God will save him with gusto. He will claim him as a son and clothe him in righteousness and rejoice over him with great joy and reserve him a seat at the marriage supper of the Lamb.

Conclusion

Prostitution is a vile business. The prostitute and the prostitute-user disgust God by their degrading and destructive activities. Yet God loves them still, and would spare them the hell they deserve. This is his grace, his unspeakable, unstinting, undeserved kindness. Let God's people declare that grace as loudly as they deplore the sin that makes the grace necessary. And let the prostitute and the prostitute-user see their sin so that they may see their need for grace, and receive it in repentance and faith to the glory of God.

---

* Although it occurs between members of the same sex, the most common form of prostitution is between men and women. This study focuses on heterosexual prostitution.

Prostitution and Social Justice

Given the overall decline of moral standards in our society, it is not surprising that moves to legalise prostitution have become almost irresistible. While most advocates of law reform stop short of saying that prostitution is good, many claim that it is harmless. It is, they say, a "victimless crime", and therefore should not be subject to legal censure.

Social justice

But prostitution is far from a "victimless" activity. The damage it causes to the well-being of a society is considerable. Indeed, it undermines social justice in at least four ways.

Firstly, prostitution demeans women by encouraging men to view them as sex objects. It separates sex from love, respect, commitment and relationship. In a brothel, a woman becomes merely a product that possesses the attributes and responses necessary to satisfy a man's physical urges. If, by frequenting a brothel, a man comes to view one woman as a sex object, what is to stop him from viewing other women likewise? Through prostitution, the dignity of all women is degraded, including that of the prostitute herself.

Secondly, prostitution undermines the institution of marriage by encouraging promiscuity among single men and adultery among married men. A single man who has frequented a brothel will find it difficult to adapt to a normal marriage relationship. (Prostitutes boast, "We will do what your wife or girlfriend won't do!")[1] Apart from that, what young wife would not be emotionally wounded by the knowledge that her husband has slept with a prostitute? For married men, the use of a prostitute constitutes adultery, which is one of the deepest betrayals of love and trust possible between two human beings. Added to the emotional degradation of adultery, the wife may find she is expected to perform in the same raunchy or perverted manner as a prostitute. Worse still, she risks contracting a range of sexually transmitted diseases, some of which are incurable, and others lethal.

Thirdly, prostitution lowers the health of the community by facilitating the spread of sexually transmitted diseases. Because of the unhygienic nature of their "work", prostitutes are constantly at risk from a range of diseases, including AIDS, hepatitis B and C, Chlamydia, genital herpes, genital warts, gonorrhoea and syphilis. Once infected, prostitutes infect their "clients", who in turn infect their wives and girlfriends.

Fourthly, prostitution impoverishes the community financially by diverting funds to health and welfare programmes. The cost of regular health checks and treatment of prostitutes is met, at least in part, from public revenue. Men who get infected from prostitutes claim on Medicare, as do the spouses they infect. When a marriage breaks up because a husband commits adultery with a prostitute, the community pays for the divorce, along with any welfare benefits needed by the broken family.

Prostitution contributes to social injustice, to say nothing of personal immorality. Far from being a "victimless" crime, it harms the whole community.

Prostitutes as victims

Attempts are often made to portray prostitutes as the victims of abuse or poverty. In contemporary thinking, to confer victim status is to exonerate from blame.

Women choose to become prostitutes, we are told, because of "a background of childhood poverty, violence and incest and the resulting low self-esteem." While there may be some truth in such a claim, how does it support the cause of law reform? Are we to believe that if a woman comes from an oppressed background she will benefit by entering an oppressive occupation? Are we to credit that if she suffers from low self-esteem she cannot be harmed by an occupation which affords her no self-esteem? Are we to think that if she has been degraded by relatives the law should permit her to be degraded by strangers?

No doubt some prostitutes come from emotionally and/or economically deprived backgrounds. It does not follow from this, however, that such disadvantages either compel women to become prostitutes or excuse women who do. Several million people in Australia—many single mothers among them—cope on low incomes without resorting to prostitution. It is an insult to these people to assert or to imply that there is a necessary or inevitable connection between poverty and prostitution.

The issue is not whether we concede that some prostitutes come from disadvantaged backgrounds. The pertinent questions are these: Is prostitution morally wrong? Is it socially harmful? If the answer to either of these questions is yes, then we must oppose attempts to liberalise prostitution laws.

The main reason women in Australia take up prostitution is money. When it comes to economics, prostitutes are not so much exploited as exploiters. For while it is true that men use prostitutes, it is equally true that prostitutes use men.

The American name for a prostitute—"hooker"—is highly descriptive in this regard. A prostitute is a woman who catches men with sex as an angler catches fish with a baited hook. She has no concern for the individual she has hooked, or the wife he may be betraying, or the family he may be breaking. Her only concern is to use him for financial gain.

In certain respects prostitutes are victims, but in other respects they are victimisers.

"Clients" as villains

One way to advance the notion that prostitutes are victims is to present their "clients" as villains. Of course, any move to vilify prostitute-users ought to be welcomed. Men who use prostitutes are guilty of personal immorality and social irresponsibility. They should be utterly condemned for their depravity.

However, condemning the client should not lead to exonerating the prostitute. A prostitute is not virtuous because her client is craven. To blame a man for being lustful does not excuse a woman for being loose. Both, in their own ways, are guilty. Both should be condemned.

Supply and demand

Another argument used to deflect criticism from prostitutes is that prostitution exists only because men want it. Without the demand, it is claimed, there would be no prostitution.

Certainly, demand affects supply. There can be no doubt that some men are debauched, and go out of their way to hire women for sex. But it can also happen the other way around. As every good advertiser knows, a well-marketed supply can create a demand.

Prostitutes are not in the "business" for personal satisfaction. Those who comment publicly about their "profession" usually indicate that they do not like men or the things men do to them. So why are they involved in prostitution? Men are in it for pleasure. But what about women? The answer is that women enter prostitution for money.

Prostitutes want money—big money, quick money, easy money—and to get it they must have clients. The more clients they solicit the more money they make. Hence, they have a vested interest in creating demand.

In many instances, the *supply* of saleable sex produces a demand for it. The more prostitutes there are and the more respectable and visible they become, the more demand for their services will increase.

If a man passes a brothel each week on his way to the fish-and-chip shop, he will be tempted to use it. This does not mean, of course, that he will inevitably succumb to the temptation, or that he would be excused if he did. But it does mean that he must continually resist a temptation to which he should never be subjected.

The man who is good simply because he does not have the opportunity to be bad has nothing to boast about. And yet he is better (and better off) than the man who does what is bad. Some men do not use prostitutes because they are not readily available. This is not praiseworthy, but it is preferable to debauchery. If brothels are legalised and consequently become both more numerous and less odious, some men who would not otherwise have done so will begin to purchase sex.

When it comes to sex, men are the weaker sex. Their desire is easily inflamed and their self-control is easily subverted. Society and governments should be mindful of this weakness, and should not allow pimps, madams and prostitutes to exploit it. It is a grave evil to do anything to cause anyone to stumble. "Woe to the man [the woman, the government] by whom the temptation comes!" (Matt 18:7).

Men at risk

Sexual desire, especially for men, has considerable and continual power. Even men with high moral standards—including Christian men—may be adversely affected by the proliferation of prostitution.

One Christian man has given an account that illustrates how easily men can be seduced by a prostitute. Writing with deep regret and without self-justification, this man recounted that he was asleep in a hotel when he was woken early in the morning by a knock on the door. He continues:

> I opened it cautiously to find an attractive blonde who spoke in a gentle but tantalising tone. She told me her name which I immediately forgot and asked if she could come in.
>
> It was obvious why she was here and I had a few seconds to consider an offer from her I *could* refuse. To my own amazement I invited her in, still considering a path of action.
>
> She sensed my hesitancy and as we sat on the bed together she caressed me and in her gentle, inviting tone reiterated her proposition. With my mind still considering a course of action, but with my senses and emotions stirred, I finally agreed to her tempting business proposition.
>
> We negotiated a price and as if in a virtual state of oblivion to my situation I collected my purchase. A purchase which was to haunt and follow me for many months.[2]

This account should alert us to three truths concerning prostitution. Firstly, the prostitute is not always a passive "victim" but rather is often an active predator. Secondly, the ready supply of prostitution increases the actual demand for it. Thirdly, even upright men free of lustful intention can fall prey to prostitutes.

Women at risk

But it is not only men who are at risk. Lenient attitudes and laws on prostitution place temptation in the way of women, too. Advertisements in the personal employment columns of daily newspapers constantly entice young women to enter prostitution. "Great money to be made," says one. "Suit any girls on holidays or in need of fast money," says another. "Earn more than anywhere else," says another. "Earn up to $800 per shift," says yet another.[3] Madams and pimps do not place these advertisements in vain. They offer young women money that cannot be matched by any other "profession".

At $800 per shift, a young woman could earn $4,000 for a five-day week—or over $200,000 per year. And she could earn it without any skills or qualifications. If she studied six years without pay at university to become a doctor, she would be unlikely to earn that amount in her seventh year.

It is hardly surprising, therefore, that some women succumb to the temptation of prostitution, with its promise of "great" and "fast" money. And even more women will fall to this temptation if prostitution is legalised. When the Western Australian government proposed to legalise prostitution in 1987, for example, Perth brothels and escort agencies reported a marked increase in the number of women enquiring about "work". "One brothel had six women applying for work on one morning", which was "more than it would usually receive in two weeks."[4]

Who are these young women who yield to the lure of prostitution? Each one is someone's daughter, someone's sister. Why not yours, mine?

We become offended when it is suggested that our daughters (or sisters) could be lured into prostitution. Why? It is because we know that prostitution is a vile, disgusting business—and we cannot bear to think of our daughters being involved in it in any way. We cannot bear to think of them being degraded by scores of depraved men.

Given that we feel this way about our own daughters, shouldn't we experience a similar outrage at the thought of other people's daughters being degraded by prostitution? If prostitution is vile for our daughters, isn't it also vile for our neighbours' daughters?

And given that *someone's* daughter is lured into prostitution every day, can we be entirely confident that *our* daughters will not be lured? Again, this is an offensive notion. *Our* daughters are decent girls. Precisely! And so, too, were once all the girls who are now prostitutes. No girl is born a prostitute. If our neighbour's daughter, who was once an innocent girl, could be enticed into prostitution, why couldn't our own daughters be similarly enticed?

Prostitution will become increasingly attractive to young women as it becomes increasingly approved. If society excuses the behaviour of prostitutes, pretending that they provide "a necessary and harmless service", and if society sanitises prostitutes themselves, pretending that they are merely "working girls" in "the world's oldest profession", then why should young women shy away from this "profession" when making their career choices? In short, if young women get the impression that to be a prostitute is really not so bad, then why should they pass up $200,000 a year in a brothel for $20,000 a year in a supermarket?

Law reform arguments

Legalising and accepting prostitution puts young women at risk. Yet advocates of law reform seem unconcerned about this. Rather, they fret about the risk to police if prostitution laws are not repealed. Police could be corrupted by having to enforce the law, they claim.

There is a potential for police corruption, of course. However, the same could be said of other laws that police have to enforce, such as those governing drug trafficking. Should governments legalise narcotic drugs because police could be "bought off" by dealers? The potential for police corruption is an argument for caution, not legalisation.

Some people argue that prostitution laws should be repealed because they are not enforced. However, governments could resolve this problem by the simple measure of instructing police to compel compliance. Governments could further help by strengthening the law, so that penalties are more severe and definitions are more precise. Small fines need to be replaced by hefty fines, and definitions need to be broadened to include "massage parlours" and "escort agencies". Governments should strengthened legislation against prostitution, then direct police to abandon containment policies and implement suppression policies.

It should be noted, however, that laws against prostitution are valuable simply because they exist. While it is preferable for laws to be enforced, the prosecution and punishment of criminals is not their only function. Laws educate citizens concerning minimum standards of acceptable behaviour. In this way they help to prevent a further decline in standards. Un-enforced laws also create an air of uncertainty for those who break them: law-breakers must keep on guessing about just how far they can go, and so they can never be quite as brazen as they might like to be. In some respects, therefore, laws do not have to be enforced to have some beneficial effect. They merely have to exist.

Some advocates of law reform argue that it is hypocritical to prosecute the prostitute but not the prostitute-user. This argument is entirely correct. The solution, however, is not to decriminalise the prostitute's activities, but to criminalise the client's. Let the law condemn the man who buys sex along with the woman who sells it!

Some people claim that legalising prostitution will allow governments to control it more effectively. Politicians who try to sell law reform legislation say things like, "We are not condoning prostitution. We are tightening up. All those brothels working outside the proposed new legislation will face severe penalties." Why should anyone believe assurances like these? If madams and prostitutes flout the existing law, why would they feel obliged to abide by new laws? And if the police are lenient on brothels when the law is strict, why would they become strict on brothels once the law is lenient?

Some who support law reform claim that legalising prostitution will help prevent the spread of sexually transmitted diseases, because new laws will mandate weekly medical checks for prostitutes. But weekly health checks, even if rigorously enforced, will not prevent the spread of sexually transmitted diseases. The symptoms of some diseases are not discernable within a week. But more importantly, a prostitute could become infected immediately after her medical examination, by the very first client she services after leaving her examining doctor, and then go on to infect every man who uses her for a full week before her next check-up uncovers her infectiousness. Unless every prostitute is examined immediately after every sexual encounter, and unless such examinations can accurately detect every sexually transmitted disease, there is no foolproof way to prevent the spread of disease through prostitution.

Arguments for prostitution law reform are flawed, and should not sway right-thinking people.

Conclusion

Prostitution subverts personal goodness and social justice. It involves private immorality and public irresponsibility. It causes individual and collective harm.

Rather than enjoy legal status and social acceptance, prostitution ought to be outlawed by any society that aspires to protect its citizens from the ravages of greed and lust.

How Pornography Harms Us

Many people believe that pornography is harmless, provided it is not linked with violence or children. Other people, however, believe that all pornography is harmful, whether or not it depicts violence and/or children. The difficulty for the second group is to explain just how pornography harms us. In this essay I hope to overcome that difficulty by identifying ten ways in which pornography harms individuals, families and communities.

I formulated these ten (often overlapping) categories of harm while reading the stories of men and women who testified before the Attorney General's Commission on Pornography in the United States.[1] Although these testimonies were given in 1985 and 1986, they are no less relevant today. In fact, the early date of the testimonies actually increases their relevance. For if pornography caused such harm in the 1980s when it was much less explicit and much less common than it is now, what devastation must it be causing among us today?

Whether "soft core" (depicting only nudity) or "hard core" (depicting also sexual acts and/or perversions), pornography harms us. It does so in the following ways:

The moral sense of men

Pornography harms the moral sensibilities of men. It destroys their ability and their desire to determine right from wrong in sexual matters.

One woman who wished to remain anonymous testified to the Commission that, after thirty years of marriage, "my husband's personality totally changed in just three months" from the time he began to watch pornography on cable television. He began staying up late at night to watch the more raunchy movies. He also began to read pornographic magazines. Then he began "trying to get me to act out what he saw on the porn movies. Each time this would end up in an argument because I found the ideas repulsive and the acts nauseous."

During this time, she clung to the hope that he "would grow out of his liking for porn." But he didn't: "what happened was that he began to look for a woman who would not be 'too good' for him. He thought I was too prudish. ... We continued to have marital relations during this period of time, but he was never again satisfied with sex once he was exposed to porn. He felt he was cheated because I wouldn't do what the TV and movie actresses did."

Within eighteen months their marriage was over: "my husband moved in with one of the loose women he chased. He demanded a divorce ... He still lives with that woman without benefit of marriage and has lost all sense of right and wrong. Before pornography came into our lives, he had always been a moral man" (pp.221-226).

This one account is sufficient to establish that pornography ruins the moral sense of the men who use it. However, much of what follows will testify to the same reality.

The moral sense of women

Pornography harms the moral sensibilities of women. It is not just men who are morally corrupted by pornography. Women are, too. Women who view pornography either lose or fail to develop an understanding of what is good, right and natural in sexual matters.

A former Playboy bunny, Brenda MacKillop states, "My first association with Playboy began in childhood when I found *Playboy* as well as other pornographic magazines hidden around the house. ... This gave me a distorted image of sexuality. ... I never questioned the morality of becoming a Playboy bunny because the magazine was accepted into the home." Brenda continues, "*Playboy* is more than a pornographic magazine with pictures of naked women. It is a philosophy that enticed me to throw aside my Judeo-Christian ethic of no premarital sex and no adultery and to practice recreational sex with no commitments" (p.91).

The moral sense of children

Pornography harms the moral sensibilities of children. Children who are exposed to pornography are corrupted by it.

Girls who view pornography come to view themselves as they are depicted in the pornography—that is, as sexual objects. As a consequence, they feel that they ought to be constantly and totally available to men for sexual purposes. To implement this availability, they then either become promiscuous (as illustrated by Brenda MacKillop in the previous example) or submissive (as illustrated by Susan Wilhem in the following example).

Susan Wilhem states, "Pornography has long been in my life. My father used soft-core pornography. ... I was not supposed to read them, but I read everything that was in the house. The magazines presented women in two ways: either the woman was a dumpy, nagging fishwife with her hair in curlers, or she was beautiful, sexy, and always available. ... Those magazines were my primary education about the roles of women in our society. ... [They] influenced my expectations about men and sexuality" (p.139). Because of the way pornography moulded her views, Susan accepted her husband's use of pornography in her marriage, and acquiesced to the degrading demands he made of her.

Boys who read pornography quickly develop a distorted view of women and of sex.

Dr Simon Miranda gives an account of a four year old boy whose father kept *Playboy* magazines and whose uncle had unwittingly let him see some sex acts on television. The result? His mother "found him in the bathroom trying to [perform a certain sex act with] the centrefold of a *Playboy* magazine" (p.219).

James Schellenberg explains that he came into contact with pornography at the age of twelve when some friends talked him into using his family's projector to screen two pornographic movies. They "showed naked men and women in various sexual acts and poses and were extremely stimulating to an about-to-become teenager." Schellenberg explains that the movies "gave me entry into the world of pornography" and "led from one thing to another. My friends and I started to collect magazines and pictures. In my junior high school years in the early fifties, the main attraction was decks of playing cards, each card showing naked men and/or women in different sexual poses and positions. The magazines we got our hands on were mild compared to what is available today [1985]. Nevertheless, we stared and lusted upon them, hour after hour." The lust for pornography continued from childhood into adulthood, utterly dominating

Shellenberg's life. He concludes, "Today, at the age of forty-eight, with four children, two boys and two girls ranging from sixteen to twenty-three, I still struggle daily with the images, the thoughts, the yearnings, the lusts cultivated during those years of self-indulgence in pornography. They are permanently embedded in my being. ... The thoughts daily affect my relationship with my wife, my daughters, and women with whom I come in contact, even in church. I am constantly repressing unhealthy thoughts and lusts, cravings and yearnings cultivated during those years. My sexual experience is not normal. My relationship with my wife and daughters is stunted" (pp.143-147).

Self-control in men

Pornography harms the will power of men. It pervades their thoughts, perverts their desires and erodes their self-control. It brings them under tremendous bondage.

Dan states how exposure to pornography at age nine brought him into a bondage from which he could not break free for the next forty years of his life. A homosexual man in his early twenties befriended him and ultimately took him to an empty railroad car. The man then "took some little cartoon books out of his pocket and showed them to me. I had never seen anything like them in my life until that day. They showed several cartoon characters in various stages of fornication and oral sex." Using the pictures to arouse both Dan and himself, the homosexual then engaged in oral sex with Dan. While Dan did not become addicted to homosexual sex, he did become addicted to pornography.

He tried to break the addiction after his marriage at age twenty-two. He disposed of his pornographic collection. And he stopped buying pornographic materials—for a while. "However, the demon which had invaded my mind in that railroad car so many years ago was not to let me alone. Without any consciousness on my part, I had been thoroughly conditioned to relate pornography with my own sexual experiences. ...

"There were periods when I was unable to concentrate my thoughts on anything other than mental images of sexually explicit material. I remember going into a newsstand to purchase a paper one day and saw the first issue of *Playboy* magazine. It was like a magnet compelling me to buy a copy. It was as though I had no choice in the matter."

The bondage began all over again. "During the sixties and seventies, I purchased thousands of explicit sex materials, including books, magazines, and 8-millimetre movies. I saw hundreds of films at adult movie theatres. I tried many times to stop my habit and would often dispose of everything I had collected. I would burn the material, hundreds, even thousands of dollars going up in smoke, only it never stopped. Eventually the urge would come over me, and it would start all over again, each time my appetite becoming more bizarre."

After forty years of addiction, Dan sought help. "I have not purchased sexually explicit material for over four years, but the demon is still there, just waiting for the opportunity to regain control, and it requires constant vigilance on my part to keep it under control. I cannot allow myself to be in a situation where I might weaken and once again fall prey to pornography. I cannot and will not patronise a store that displays and sells any type of sexually oriented material. I must carefully select the television programs I watch and the movies I see. Sometimes I am caught off guard. When someone leaves a copy of *Playboy* or *Penthouse* lying around, I must leave as quickly as possible, because I know if I took so much as one little peek, it would start all over again, and I cannot afford to let that happen" (pp.161-164).

Many people defend pornography on the grounds of freedom—the freedom of individuals to view and do whatever they please. Ironically, those who exercise that freedom end up in slavery.

Self-esteem in women

Pornography harms the emotions and self-esteem of women. A wife whose husband uses pornography finds herself burdened by impossible expectations concerning appearance and performance. She is soon wounded by unfavourable comparisons with ever-young "models" and degraded by insistent requests for unusual and perverse sexual favours.

Ironically, while pornography encourages a man to be dissatisfied with his wife's appearance, it also encourages him to demand more of her sexually. The porn models may be more beautiful than his wife, but she is more available than them. So he comes to expect her to satisfy his inflamed and perverted appetite. He expects her to perform the same acts pictured in the pornography.

Speaking of her ex-husband, Susan Wilhem states, "He had a lot of pornography around the house, both slicks and the hard core ... He frequently suggested that our sex life would be more fun if I would be willing to try some of the things he saw pictured in the magazines. He often told me that our sex life and I were dull, blah, and awful ... Once we saw an X-rated film that showed [a certain sex act]. After that, he insisted that I try [it]. I agreed to do so, trying to be the available, willing creature that I thought I was supposed to be. I found the experience very painful, and I told him so. But he kept insisting that we try it again and again. He reinforced his insistence with verbal abuse" (pp.139-140).

Bonnie says of her second husband, "Paul had a large collection of bizarre S&M and bondage pornography that he kept in the night-stand drawer in our bedroom. On one occasion Paul tied me to our bed and sodomized me. This occurred after I refused to agree to be bound and tied as the models appeared in some of Paul's pornographic magazines. Many times I would be asked by Paul to accompany him either to an X-rated porn movie or one of the adult book stores. I would vehemently say no. He often requested me to either pose nude in a very obscene way or asked me to look at his porno books. Many times he would show me pornographic pictures and say, 'Why don't you do this?' or 'Pose like this'" (p.36).

Rape or worse

Pornography harms not only the emotional, but also the physical, wellbeing of women. It increases the incidence of rape.

Evelyn states that her husband "would go to massage parlours, prostitutes, and X-rated movies. Then he would come and tell me about it; then he would get angry because I wouldn't have sex with him. He would force himself on me many times. Sometimes five times a night—I guess you would call that rape" (p.90).

Noting that a man had attempted to rape a certain Playmate of the Year after he recognised her from *Playboy* magazine, Brenda MacKillop states, "Obviously this man had the idea that centrefolds who appear nude in the magazines he reads want to be his sexual playmates. I believe many women are raped due to this impression given by pornography that all women want to be used sexually" (pp.92-93).

A magazine centrefold at least has a choice about whether or not to allow herself to be viewed by men in explicitly sexual terms. But unsuspecting women who encounter men aroused by the centrefold do not. Evelyn (above) had no choice. Nor did a thirteen-year-old girl who went for a stroll one day in a forest. She came across "a group of hunters reading pornography. As they saw her, one said, 'There's a live one.' They gang-raped her for several hours" (p.126).

Thomas Schiro raped over twenty women before he was caught and sentenced to death for the rape and strangulation of a young woman in Indiana in 1981. According to Dr Frank Osanka, who spent fifty clinical hours evaluating Schiro before his trial, "Thomas Schiro's first exposure to pornography happened before he was eight years old. He discovered two of his father's World War II vintage pornography films. Viewing the films motivated him to masturbate and develop a need for exposure to additional pornography. One of the films was entitled *Bedtime* and illustrated a man and a woman engaged in a variety of sexual interactions. The significant aspect of the film was the depiction of the woman's body as being sexually enthusiastic, while at the same time the camera frequently drew attention to her anguished facial features. The message to young Schiro was that women enjoy sexually related pain. Later he learned that most women did not enjoy such pain and humiliation, but by that time he did not care because he had developed sadistic needs to hurt women, either in thoughts or actions" (p.105).

It is naïve to claim, as some do, that pornography saves women from rape. Pornography does not provide an outlet for a man's sexual urges. On the contrary, it arouses those urges, which then require a "live" woman for an outlet.

And, horrendously, the live woman may be a dead woman once the rapist has finished with her. For when pornography leads to rape it can easily lead on to murder. Thomas Schiro illustrates this, and he is not alone. Other men have murdered women and children as a result of using pornography. Perhaps the most famous of these pornography-motivated killers is Ted Bundy. In the 1980s he raped and murdered 28 women, the last being only 12 years old. Before his execution in 1989, Bundy confessed that pornography was the thing that kindled and fuelled his deadly lust. He also claimed that pornography played a major part in the lives and crimes of the other murderers he knew on death row.[2]

Of course, murder is the most extreme and the least likely harm to arise from the use of pornography. However, this is little comfort for Ted Bundy's 28 victims and their families. Murder following rape is pornography's ultimate harm. Let there be just one Bundy for every ten million men who use pornography, and we have a compelling case against pornography.

Child sexual abuse

Pornography contributes to the problem of child sexual abuse. It does so in three ways. Firstly, the production of child pornography requires the sexual abuse of the children depicted in that pornography. Secondly, that same pornography arouses lust towards children in adult viewers, who then abuse children for sexual satisfaction. Thirdly, that same pornography is also used by paedophiles to lure children into sexual activity.

Bonnie explains that her first husband, Leon, used pornography that included depictions of "small children in various acts of sex and violence." She continues, "Once when I went to bingo across the street with my mother, he tied both of my daughters to their beds on their stomachs and [indecently assaulted them]. When Debbie and Michelle told me, I believed them immediately because Leon had done the same to me before."

Sadly, Bonnie's second husband was also addicted to pornography and also sexually abused her children. Referring to a particular incident, Bonnie states, "I feel that the bathroom molestation can be linked to some of the child pornography that Paul possessed which depicted young nude females in bathtubs in sexually provocative poses. My daughters told me that Paul asked them if they wanted to pose like the girls in the magazines and to be photographed."

Bonnie concludes her sad account: "My beautiful daughters are very wary and fearful of men now, and Michelle still suffers from headaches, nightmares, and doesn't like to walk anywhere alone. … Both Debbie and Michelle say quite often they don't want to get married or date when they are old enough" (p.35-38).

Bonnie's husband, Paul, illustrates how child pornography can be used to break down the modesty and inhibitions of children. By showing his stepdaughters pictures of naked girls in sexual poses, Paul was showing them that other girls do the very things that he wanted them to do. So it must be all right, mustn't it?

But child pornography is not the only material paedophiles use to seduce children. Adult pornography serves the purpose just as well. A sixteen-year-old girl, Garrett Gilbert states, "I was about ten years old when I was first exposed to pornography. The man who introduced pornography to me was a long-time trusted friend of the family". The material he used? "They were magazines like *Playboy* and *Penthouse*." Over a period of weeks, viewing the pornography led to fondling and then to a variety of other sexual activities. When Garrett was eleven and a half, the man, a lawyer, began to expose her to hard core adult pornography. "It was these magazines that he started having me act out positions with him" (pp.206-208). Then he began to photograph her.

Garrett's mother, Judy Gilbert, explains that when the lawyer was found out and arrested, the police discovered video and audio tapes that he had made of his sexual exploits with Garrett. She continues, "I heard one of those tapes. It was a tape where you could hear the turning of the pages of a magazine and him describing to my daughter the various individuals depicted engaging in various forms and positions of sexual acts. He used this magazine to get her to do the same type of thing to him and as a tool to instruct her as to how he wanted her to pose for his nude photographs" (p.211).

Abortion

Pornography increases the incidence of abortion. Women influenced by pornography become sexually promiscuous. Promiscuity leads to unwanted pregnancy. Unwanted pregnancy leads to abortion.

Brenda MacKillop states, "In order to avoid any responsibility for an irresponsible lifestyle, abortion is necessary. ... I will never forget a conversation between two bunnies that went something like this: First Bunny: I thought I had the flu last week, but I was pregnant. So I had an abortion. Second Bunny: Did it bother you to have the abortion? First Bunny: Well, the first time it did, but this is my third or fourth abortion, and there is no way I could take care of a child. Besides, I think I am doing the right thing by not bringing an unwanted child into the world. Second Bunny: I know what you mean. I was married and pregnant by another married man, and there is no way I could have had that baby" (p.95).

Pornography brings death into love's heartland. Because it encourages sex without affection and commitment, children conceived through its influence

171

are not wanted and are therefore subject to termination.

Virility

Pornography harms men's virility. Ultimately, it weakens the very potency that it awakens. It inflames appetite but quenches ability. It places sex in the realm of fantasy, where women are perfectly beautiful and unreservedly willing. But in real life, few women match this fantasy. So actual sex with an actual woman becomes a disappointment. By making of sex an unattainable fantasy, pornography creates a dependency upon itself.

Bonnie states, "My first husband, Leon, obtained a substantial collection of pornographic material. ... He could not perform sexually with me without first getting aroused by looking at pornography" (p.35).

As for the serial rapist Thomas Schiro, psychologist Frank Osanka states that such was the strength of his addiction that "he could not achieve an erection in any sexual act unless he coupled this desired behaviour with viewing pornography. He would often place centrefolds next to the head of his [rape] victim and demand that she lie perfectly still" (p.106).

What a cruel but appropriate irony: pornography extinguishes the very desire it ignites!

Family relationships

Lastly, pornography harms family relationships. Nothing can destroy the affection a wife has for her husband or a child has for his/her father so quickly as pornography. Many of the accounts already cited bear out the fact that pornography ruins homes. This last testimony demonstrates that even *soft core* pornography can serve the purpose.

Christine Currie states, "I remember the first time I saw pornography. It was a *Playboy* calendar. The model was young, looking seductive and completely naked. I was eleven years old. My first impression was that this was a 'girl,' not a 'woman.' She resembled me more than my mother. How hurt my mother must be that my father displays a younger woman's body in their bedroom. I felt sorry for her. It was like ageing is a reality for women and men turned their eyes. As for me, I felt embarrassed, humiliated, ashamed, and shocked. I couldn't believe anyone would put a naked girl on something so trivial as a calendar. These feelings I felt were the same feelings I would feel when my father would come into my bedroom and molest me while he thought I was asleep. My head had been spinning ever since my molestations with the word 'why?' The calendar gave me my answer.

"When my father was finally confronted by my mother, I told him there was something he could do to make me feel better. I told him to please take down the calendar. He did. I felt back then that it had set my father up to view me as sexual, and I believe this today.

"From age eleven to eighteen every day my thoughts revolved around not being around my dad. School was secondary. I was a top student before my molesting. I didn't want to tell my mother, because I knew it would hurt her. I was right, but I did not realize that I would lose her emotional support for the rest of my life. She became jealous of me. I was her competition. My father seems genuinely sorry for what happened. But back when I was going through my teens, every day was painful for me. Your faith in God is murdered. Your faith that your mother and father love you is gone …" (pp.131-132).

Conclusion: several safeguards

Given the magnitude and malignancy of pornography's ten-fold violence against men, women and children, it is imperative that we do all we can to protect ourselves and our loved ones from it. In conclusion, let me suggest several practical safeguards—first to men, then to women.

To men:

Firstly, do not be complacent. It would be a mistake to think that because you are not presently troubled by pornography you are immune from temptation. "But watch yourself, or you also may be tempted" (Gal 6:1, NIV).

Secondly, watch what you watch. Be careful what you view on television, on video, on the internet, and at the cinema. Be careful where you look when you are in the newsagency. Be careful how you look at women other than your wife. "I made a covenant with my eyes not to look lustfully at a girl" (Job 31:1).

Thirdly, take pleasure in your wife. Let her be the focus of your sexual desires, and let those desires be expressed with decency and tenderness, so that physical pleasure and emotional intimacy always keep company with each other. "Drink water from your own cistern … rejoice in the wife of your youth. A loving doe, a graceful deer—may her breasts satisfy you always, may you ever be captivated by her love" (Prov 5:15-19).

Fourthly, if you are single and unsatisfied, ask the Lord for a wife. Marriage is the place for sexual gratification. "Now to the unmarried and the widows I say: It is good for them to stay unmarried, as I am. But if they cannot control themselves, they should marry, for it is better to marry than to burn with passion" (1 Cor 7:8-9).

To women:

Firstly, be affectionate to your husband and encourage his sexual advances. Let your love be his protection and satisfaction. "I am a wall, and my breasts are like towers. Thus I have become in his eyes like one bringing contentment" (Song of Solomon 8:10).

Secondly, be aware that, for men, the temptations of pornography are pervasive and powerful. Be on guard on your husband's behalf. "She does him good, and not harm, all the days of her life" (Prov 31:12).

Thirdly, be careful not to display yourself sexually in public. Don't inadvertently adopt or reinforce the perspectives of pornography by the way you dress. Let your sensual beauty be for your husband's eyes alone. "I also want women to dress modestly, with decency and propriety" (1 Tim 2:9).

If Christian men and women attend to these basics in matters of sexual love and morality, they will shield themselves from the harm of pornography and open themselves to the pleasure of sex in all purity, to the good of their families and the glory of God.

Obsessed with Sex?

I recently spoke with a Western Australian Labor Party politician concerning the new Labor government's proposals to lower the age of consent for homosexuals from 21 to 16 and to compel acceptance of homosexuality through anti-discrimination legislation.

During the course of what was a courteous and constructive discussion, the politician expressed a conviction that there were more important social issues to address than the one we were discussing. The MP also expressed concern that Christians seem to be obsessed with sex.

I replied that Christians are deeply concerned about sexual morality because they recognise that sexual and social matters are interlinked. Through homosexuality, prostitution and adultery, diseases are spread, marriages are broken, sensibilities are perverted and lives are ruined. Sexual immorality is one of the major causes of social injustice in our society today. Christians have the wisdom to see this.

I also asked if it would be fair to say that the Labor Party is obsessed with sex. After all, it was ministers of the Gallop Labor Government who *in the first week after the election* announced the new government's intention to introduce laws to advance the practice of homosexuality and prostitution in Western Australia. And this does not take into account a pre-election promise by the now Minister for Police that a new Labor government would legislate to allow skimpy barmaids to wear G-strings and see-through tops in places such as Kalgoorlie-Boulder.[1]

Well, I guess the new government has things other than sex on its mind. But given its rush to draft laws to allow men to sodomise each other at a younger age and to buy women in brothels and to ogle women in pubs, we could be forgiven for thinking that Labor MPs are obsessed with sex. And it is a dirty, destructive obsession that, for love of God and neighbour, Christians must resist.

We want people to know that sex is God's good gift to us, a gift that binds families together and strengthens society when it is enjoyed between one man and one woman in a loving marriage relationship. We want to warn people that sex in any other context brings guilt, strife and even (through abortion, AIDS and jealous rage) death.

So, thanks to the initiatives of the new government, Christians must yet again express concern about the personal and social dangers of sexual immorality. As a consequence, we will yet again suffer the outrageous slander that it is *we*, not *they*, who are obsessed with sex.

How Green Is God?

From childhood I have loved the natural world—and Australian wildlife and wilderness in particular. When I was a boy I used to read nature books and magazines, keep finches and quails, collect eggs and shells, and catch lizards and ant-lions. From adulthood I have continually celebrated the wonders of nature in my poetry.[1]

As a Christian drawn to nature, I am keen to know what God has to say about it in his word, the Bible. How important is the natural world in its own right? How important is it in relation to human beings? How should it be used and/or conserved? How does the green movement fit with the Christian faith? In short, how green is God?[2]

God cares for nature

The Bible teaches that God created the universe and everything in it. The galaxies did not originate from a chance explosion of matter; and life did not originate from the random combination of inorganic substances. On the contrary, God made the earth and filled it with innumerable living things, both great and small. By his will, wisdom and power all things were created and have their being.[3]

After he had finished his mighty acts of creation, "God saw everything that he had made, and behold, it was very good" (Gen 1:31). His creation was perfect, and it delighted him.

Now it stands to reason that if God created the earth's flora and fauna, and if he is pleased with them, then he must have an interest in them and a concern for them. Scripture confirms what reason contends.

God's care for his creatures is demonstrated by his detailed knowledge of them. He declares, "I know all the birds of the air, and all that moves in the field is mine" (Ps 50:11). To emphasise his supreme knowledge of his entire creation, God asked Job: "Do you know when the mountain goats bring forth? Do you observe the calving of the hinds? Do you give the horse his might? Is it by your wisdom that the hawk soars? Is it at your command that the eagle mounts up?" (Job 39: 1, 19, 26, 27). The Lord Jesus Christ told his disciples that such is God's interest in, and involvement with, his creation that not even a sparrow falls to the ground without his knowledge and permission (Matt 10:29).

God's care for his creatures is also demonstrated by his provision for them. Jesus said: "Look at the birds of the air: they neither sow nor reap nor gather into barns, and yet your heavenly Father feeds them" (Matt 6:26). God sustains his creatures by supplying their needs. Again God asked Job, "Who provides for the raven its prey, when its young ones cry to God, and wander about for lack of food?" (38:41). Who is moved to pity when the fledgling ravens cry out in hunger? God is! Who provides food for them in their plight? God does! This fact is all the more remarkable when we appreciate that under Old Testament law the raven was viewed as an unclean bird, a bird which the people of Israel were not allowed to eat, or even to touch (Lev 11:13, 15, 24). This unclean bird, this bird of no practical value, is the object of God's tender care. Similarly, "The young lions roar for their prey, seeking their food from God" (Ps 104:21). Indeed, all creatures look to God, "to give them their food in due season" (Ps 104:27).

God's care for his creatures is additionally demonstrated by his protection of them. The Old Testament contains certain guidelines for the preservation of the environment and its wildlife. For example, God rules out the wanton destruction of vegetation, as indicated in Deuteronomy 20:19, where he commands the people of Israel, "When you besiege a city for a long time, making war against it in order to take it, you shall not destroy its trees by wielding an axe against them; for you may eat of them, but you shall not cut them down. Are the trees in the field men that they should be besieged by you?" Trees enjoy a measure of divine protection. And so do the birds that nest in them. For God commands the hunter: "If you chance to come upon a bird's nest, in any tree or on the ground, with young ones or eggs and the mother sitting upon the young or upon the eggs, you shall not take the mother with the young; you shall let the mother go" (Deut 22:6-7). Even a mother bird is safeguarded by our Father God!

God also extends protection to domestic animals. He commands, for example, "You shall not muzzle an ox when it treads out the grain" (Deut 25:4). In ancient times, oxen were yoked to wooden sledges which they pulled around the threshing floor to break up the stalks and husks of the grain in preparation for winnowing. To prevent an ox from eating the grain, a farmer would cover or tie up its mouth. But the Lord forbade this, insisting that the animal should be allowed to eat as it worked. Kindness towards domestic animals is pleasing to God. Proverbs 12:10 states that "A righteous man has regard for the life of his beast". One of the ways a person shows consideration for his animal is to ease its labour. Hence, God commands, "Six days you shall do your work, but on the seventh day you shall rest; that your ox and your ass may have rest" (Exod 23:12).

God's care for his creatures is further demonstrated by his approval of the study of them. He "gave Solomon wisdom and understanding beyond measure". With this wisdom, Solomon spoke, among other things, "of trees, from the cedar that is in Lebanon to the hyssop that grows out of the wall; he spoke also of beasts, and birds, and of reptiles, and of fish" (1 Kings 4:33). Inspired by God, Israel's third king became a great naturalist. He also carved "palm trees and open flowers" in various places in the temple he built for the Lord (1 Kings 6:29, 32, 35), thereby intimating that the natural world is precious to God and contributes to his praise.

The magnitude of God's love for all his creatures, great and small, is celebrated in Psalm 84:3, which exclaims: "Even the sparrow finds a home, and the swallow a nest for herself, where she may lay her young, at your altars, O LORD of hosts, my King and my God." This tender picture shows that God's concern for his creatures is not business-like but father-like, not distant but nearby, not general but particular. Even the most insignificant of his creatures is welcome in his presence.

The earth's plants and animals are precious to God. He is intensely interested in, and intimately involved with, the life of each one of them. He knows their natures and calls them all by name. He supplies their needs and protects their interests. In this respect, he is the Cosmic Conservationist, the Original Greenie.

God gave humans dominion over nature

However, so far as an understanding of mankind's relationship to nature is concerned, God is at odds with many of today's conservationists.

God made the natural world for his own pleasure and to reveal his own glory. But he also made it for mankind's pleasure and profit. At the end of the six days of creation, he instructed Adam and Eve to "Be fruitful and multiply, and fill the earth and subdue it; and have dominion over the fish of the sea and over the birds of the air and over every living thing that moves upon the earth" (Gen 1:28). This command does not sanction the destruction of the environment; but it does permit, and even require, the wise use of natural resources for the benefit of mankind.

Many conservationists misunderstand what the Bible means when it speaks of human dominion over nature. They define dominion in terms of degradation and destruction. But such notions have nothing to do with the biblical concept of dominion. As already noted, God's love for the earth and its creatures is boundless. In this regard, he out-greens the greens to an infinite degree! So he plainly was not telling Adam and Eve to degrade or destroy the earth's creatures and their habitat. He was not setting up a dictatorship but a guardianship. He intended human beings to administer and utilise the natural world benevolently.

Mankind's dominion over nature involves the legitimate use of natural things. For example, to split a tree into posts is to have dominion over nature. To fence a piece of land for pasture is to have dominion over nature. To keep a sheep in a paddock is to have dominion over nature. To shear wool from a sheep is to have dominion over nature. We could go on and on. To keep dogs for pets, to pen poultry for eggs, to arrange plants for gardens, to prune vines for grapes—these simple and sensible acts are acts of dominion.

While conservationists may object to the notion of human dominion over nature, they, like all people, necessarily dominate nature in numerous ways. Even the most dedicated greenie must subdue creation to live. He might object to the logging of native forests, but he is pleased to have jarrah floor-boards and furnishings in his own house. He might not wear furs, but he does wear leather sandals cut from the hides that come from the slaughter yard. He might not eat meat, but he does eat other living things, such as carrots and turnips, and thinks nothing of hoeing the vegetable patch to kill the weeds. In short, he does what the Bible says he ought to do: he subdues the earth for his own survival.

Dominion involves more than consumption, however. It also involves conservation. The right to exploit is counterbalanced by the responsibility to protect. Dominion in this sense is necessary for the well-being of nature itself. To keep cattle for meat so game can be spared, to plant trees for timber so native forests can be preserved, to lay baits for foxes so numbats can breed up, to licence marroning in rivers so marron can remain plentiful, to study diseases in koalas so the species can survive—these are some of the ways that human beings exercise dominion over nature for nature's good.

Nature can benefit from mankind's dominion in another way. Under human guidance, plants and animals can be lifted above their natural state. For example, a dog that has been trained to round up the sheep has become something more than it would otherwise have been. Its existence is touched with added purpose. Similarly, a fruit tree that is fertilised and pruned becomes something better than it would have been in its wild state.

God charged mankind with the government of the natural world. In doing this, he conferred on humans the right to use considerately all living things. While conservationists may object to this right, even they cannot help but exercise it.

God values humans above nature

God and the greens are often at odds on a second, more serious matter concerning mankind's relationship to nature. This disagreement centres on an estimation of the comparative worth of humans and animals.

Some time ago the Australian Conservation Foundation published a brochure about endangered animals. It was an interesting and informative leaflet; but it contained one statement that demonstrated just how far conservationist and Christian thought can be from each other. It said that we must look upon all species "as our companions on planet Earth, commanding equal respect." The phrase, *commanding equal respect* hints at the idea that seems to underlie much conservationist thought today—namely, that animal life is as inherently valuable as human life.

The belief that humans are no more valuable than other animals arises from the belief that humans are basically the same as other animals; and this belief arises from the evolutionary theory, which teaches that humans evolved from other animals. Evolutionists insist that "No single, essential difference separates

181

human beings from the other animals".[4] This is an extraordinary claim, and one that defies reality. Human beings are remarkably different from "the other animals", as indicated by such intangible qualities as conscience, reason, faith, will, imagination, ambition, language, laughter, wonder and worship. These qualities find no counterpart in nature but are unique to human beings; and they arise from the fact that God made us in his own likeness so that we might enjoy a special relationship with him.

At first glance, the attempt to attribute equal value to human and animal life seems to ennoble animal life. But on closer consideration we discover that it does no such thing. Rather, it demeans human life. To say that a rabbit-eared bandicoot is as valuable as a human being does not dignify the bandicoot as much as degrade the human. We see this degrading of human life under Hinduism in India, where animal life is considered sacred. In that country, cows are permitted to eat crops while people starve.

To value all life as equal ultimately leads to a contempt for human life. *Equal* respect for animals and humans soon turns into *greater* respect for animals. D.H. Lawrence illustrates this in his poem, "Mountain Lion", which he wrote after meeting two hunters carrying a dead lion in the Lobo Canyon in Mexico. Having expressed his grief and anger over the killing, Lawrence continues:

> I think in this empty world [of the Lobo Canyon] there was room for me
> and a mountain lion.
> And I think in the world beyond [the Canyon], how easily we might spare
> a million or two of humans
> And never miss them.
> Yet what a gap in the world, the missing white frost-face of that slim
> yellow mountain lion!

Whatever their merit as poetry, these lines express a shocking devaluation of human life. Lawrence would happily sacrifice (not himself but) one or two million human beings for the life of the mountain lion. For in his thinking, a lion is special, while humans are common; a lion is rare, while humans are numerous; a lion is lovely, while humans are unlovely: so what could be more sensible than to value the lion's life *above* human life?

Now, a Christian can share with Lawrence a sense of loss and indignation over the slaughter of the rare and beautiful "slim yellow mountain lion". But no Christian should share his view that the world could easily "spare a million or two of humans" in exchange for the lion.

The notion that other forms of life are as valuable as, or even more valuable than, human life is utterly rejected by Christianity. The Lord Jesus repeatedly stressed the surpassing value of human life in God's eyes. On one occasion he exclaimed, "Of how much more value is a man than a sheep!" (Matt 12:12). On another occasion, having noted that God feeds the birds, he said, "Of how much more value are you than the birds!" (Luke 12:24). On another occasion, having noted that God cares even for the common sparrows, Jesus emphasised God's special care for human beings by saying, "Fear not, therefore; you are of more value than many sparrows" (Matt 10:31). On yet another occasion, Jesus calmed his listeners' anxieties concerning their daily necessities by saying, "Consider the lilies ... even Solomon in all his glory was not arrayed like one of these. But if God so clothes the grass of the field ... will he not much more clothe you" (Matt 6:28-30)? While God cares for the lilies and clothes them with beauty, he cares for humans and their needs even more.

In the estimation of our Creator, human life is the most valuable life on earth. In fact, it is vastly more valuable than all other life put together. Not all the rain forests, not all the seal pups, not all the great whales, not all the mountain lions, equal the value of one human soul. This truth might seem outrageous when we compare the worth of the whales against the worth of a person whom we do not like or know. But it becomes rather wonderful if we compare it with the worth of either our own life or the life of someone we love. How wonderful it is to know that the God who made all things, loves and values each one of us above all things!

Some people claim that this Christian view of the pre-eminent worth of human life is parochial (ie, narrow and bigoted), while others say that it is anthropomorphic (ie, man-centred and selfish). But it is not either of these things, for it is God's doing, not ours. He has chosen to make us in his own likeness, thereby elevating us far above other living things. He has chosen to set his special love upon us. He has chosen to send his Son to save us from sin and judgment. We had nothing to do with it.

Indeed, we are entirely astonished that it should be so. Like King David, we find ourselves saying, "When I look at your heavens, the work of your fingers, the moon and the stars which you have established; what is man that you are mindful of him, and the son of man that you care for him?" (Ps 8:3-4). Given the vastness of the universe, how can it be that God thinks about us at all? How can it be that he cares for us above and beyond everything else he has made? We do not have the answer. We only know that it is true.

The ultimate proof of the surpassing worth of mankind is found in the incarnation, when the Son of God became the man Jesus and dwelt among us. He became one of us—not one of the animals, but one of *us*—to bear our sins on the cross. The Bible teaches that all creation will ultimately benefit from Christ's death and resurrection (Rom 8:21). But this, in a sense, is by the way. For essentially "Christ Jesus came into the world to save sinners" (1 Tim 1:15). The Lord Jesus came to earth to take away our sins by dying on our behalf. This is the measure of our worth!

Conclusion

How green is God? When it comes to a love for all living things, he is greener than the greenest greenie. For he cares deeply for his creatures, watching over them constantly to ensure their welfare. However, when it comes to a love for all human beings, God is not green in the least. For he gives humans dominion over nature, and values human life above plant and animal life to an immeasurable degree.

Christians should cultivate an interest in the things of nature and strive for their conservation. This is one way to honour God and to learn more about him. But we should take care that we do not devalue human beings in the process. Rather, we should remember that people are more precious than wilderness and wildlife, not only because God created them in *his* likeness, but because he sent his Son in *their* likeness.

To help us keep a right perspective, we would do well to remember that nature is transient, while humans are eternal. On the Day of Judgment, "the earth and the works that are upon it will be burned up" (2 Pet 3:10). But human souls will not. The soul will live forever in a new, resurrection body. Persons who have placed their trust in the Lord Jesus Christ will live upon "a new earth in which righteousness dwells" (2 Pet 3:13). On this new earth all nature will be restored to its original vigour, harmony and beauty. This is the ultimate hope for every nature-lover.

Sympathy for a Shark

It could have been a scene from a horror movie—a man in the water, the water stained with blood, a shark rolling in the stain. But it was, in fact, a scene from real life at Cottesloe Beach in Western Australia.

On Monday morning, 6 November 2000, a white pointer shark attacked a swimmer, tearing his leg off. The victim, Ken Crew, quickly bled to death.

The attack was terrifying, the death was tragic, but the community reaction was extraordinary.

The first extraordinary thing was that the authorities from the Fisheries Department did not immediately kill the shark. They could have done so easily, because they had it under surveillance from boats and helicopters for more than an hour after the attack. But instead of hunting it, they merely tried to drive it out to deep water. They justified their reluctance to kill the shark on the grounds that white pointers are a protected species.

Towards the end of the day, the WA government issued an order to kill the shark. By this time the Fisheries officers did not know where the shark was—and they did not seem to want to know. They said they would not actively pursue it, and would kill it only if it returned to metropolitan beaches.

The second extraordinary thing was that the public overwhelmingly supported the inaction of the Fisheries Department. The day after Mr Crew's death, there was a massive outpouring of sympathy for the shark. The *West Australian* newspaper featured a page of emotional letters in defence of the shark.[1] Here are some excerpts:

- it is an absolute tragedy that an order has been given to kill the shark. Every time an attack is reported we hear the same story: kill the sharks—mainly from people with streak [*sic*] and nothing better to do. If we do kill all the sharks, what happens the next time someone dies of a snake bite? Kill all the snakes?

- How dare anyone, let alone a government department that is supposed to protect a species, call for the killing of the shark that attacked at Cottesloe. I am a regular diver and I love the ocean environment. I use it knowing that I am entering their domain.

- What right has Monty House [the Fisheries Minister] to order the killing of a shark? The attack was a tragedy but entering the domain of sharks is the risk one takes. Let's not mess about, Mr House. Order the slaughter of all sharks.

- I am outraged and disgusted by the reaction from various sections of the community. Have we forgotten that the ocean is the sharks' domain, not ours? ... How dare we even consider taking a shark's life when we take so many of our own. If this shark is killed, then all arguments against capital punishment become invalid.

- However tragic the death of this man is to his family and the Perth community, the shark responsible does not deserve to be killed as well. This will only cause another tragedy. The shark is a natural killer, its nature is to attack ... Sharks have every right to live in their natural environment.

- I believe that it is wrong for anyone to hunt down this so-called killer shark. These swimmers were in its domain. Who are we to say that we can hunt down and eliminate other species that may pose a threat to us? Humans are much more of a threat to the shark, and the last of these magnificent animals should be protected at all costs.

- How could we blame and kill the shark which killed the Cottesloe swimmer? The shark was protecting its territory and needing a feed.

Setting aside the exaggerations and the tone of self-righteous indignation, several errors of thought recur in these letters.

One error involves the claim that the ocean is the shark's domain, not ours. While the first half of this assertion is true, the second is not. In reality, the whole earth is mankind's domain. Human beings routinely use the ocean to swim, dive, boat, farm and fish. And we have a right to do this. So if we must share the sea with the sharks, then it follows that the sharks must share the sea with us. And as they lack our ability to think logically and act morally, they must sometimes be persuaded to share by force.

Another error involves the idea that we just have to accept the risk of shark attack if we want to enter the ocean. If we followed this logic in other matters of sea safety, we would get rid of lifesavers on the beach and life jackets in boats. After all, anyone who goes swimming runs a risk of drowning, as does anyone who goes boating—we just have to accept it! Of course, many activities involve risk. Yet one mark of being human is the desire and the ability to reduce risk. One sensible way to reduce the risk of shark attack is to kill a killer shark.

Another error involves the notion that human beings are not superior to sharks. This notion is self-evidently false. Forget about matters of moral perception, artistic expression, personal aspiration and scientific investigation for a moment. Think purely in terms of food chains and power. Even in solely ecological and biological terms, human beings are manifestly superior to sharks. We are at the top of the food chain, as a visit to any fish-and-chip shop will attest. Furthermore, we are superior in intelligence and power, as illustrated by our circling the Cottesloe shark in boats and helicopters while debating whether or not we should (rather than could) kill it. So then, the question is not whether or not we are superior. It is whether or not we should use our superiority to kill a shark.

Yet another error involves the notion that sharks should be protected *at all costs*. Let us frankly admit, however, that this claim means *at all costs to Mr Crew* (or someone else like him). It does not mean *at all costs to me*. Not one of the pro-shark letter-writers would willingly forfeit his (or her) life for a shark's. Let any one of them find himself in Mr Crew's predicament, and he would, if he could, kill the shark in an instant rather than let his leg be ripped off and his lifeblood gush into the sea. With the exception of a few whose spirits are utterly broken, all human beings hold their own lives precious. As we value our own lives we should also value the lives of others. This is part of Jesus' great teaching of doing unto others what you would have them do unto you.

God's word, the Bible, teaches that human beings are the most precious of all God's earthly creatures, because they alone bear the image of God and they alone are represented (by the Man Jesus) in the Godhead.

So it is not surprising that the Bible has something in principle to say about situations such as the one on Cottesloe Beach. Exodus 21:28 states, "If a bull gores a man or a woman to death, the bull must be stoned to death". It is fair to say that what is true for a bull is true for any other animal, including a shark. If any animal kills a human being, it must be put to death.

This commandment to the people of Israel is based upon the universal principal stated in Genesis 9:5: "And for your lifeblood I will surely demand an accounting. I will demand an accounting from every animal. And from each man, too, I will demand an accounting for the life of his fellow man." God will not tolerate the killing of innocent human beings, whether the killers are humans or animals. He will hold them to account at the cost of their blood— and (as Genesis 9:6 indicates) he requires us to do the same.

Evolution?

Until the nineteenth century most people held the view that life originated by design from God. But in the twentieth century many people adopted the view that life originated by chance from matter. The theory of evolution is responsible for this dramatic shift.

Many people believe evolution is scientific. Some believe it is compatible with creation. Others believe it is consistent with reality. I want to question each of these beliefs.

Is evolution based on science?

The great advantage evolution has over creation is that it is perceived to be scientific. But is it? Certainly, creation is a faith position: it depends on assumptions that cannot be verified by scientific method. But is evolution any different?

To determine whether evolution is based on fact or faith, we must examine its premises to see if they are proven or unproven. A premise is an assumption upon which an argument stands, and the evolutionary theory has two. The first is that life originated from inanimate matter, while the second is that the diverse species originated from a common ancestor.

Evolution's first fundamental premise is "spontaneous generation". This term conveys the idea that life generated itself from inorganic substances through a spontaneous process. Or to quote the Australian Academy of Science, "spontaneous generation" is a process by which "pieces of non-living material ... somehow become living of their own accord".[1]

The decisive thing about this premise is that science cannot show it to be true. There is no empirical evidence (that is, evidence gained on the basis of experimentation) to verify it. On the contrary, since the time of Louis Pasteur,

190

there is overwhelming empirical evidence against it.

Indeed, the Australian Academy of Science says that "There is no reason to believe that spontaneous generation can occur today". Yet the Academy encourages people to believe that it did occur in the past. Why? Because "the earth of 5000 million years ago was a very different place from what it is today. One most profound difference, of course, was the absence of consumers seeking food."[2]

What curious logic! How does the absence of consumers seeking food help non-living material to become living of its own accord? The reason there were no consumers 5000 million years ago is because there was no life! Yet the Academy would have us believe that the absence of life was a useful condition for the spontaneous generation of life. This is hardly the stuff of science, is it? It is hardly objective, verifiable fact.

Spontaneous generation is a fundamental premise of evolutionary theory. Yet it has not been—nor can it ever be—verified by science. It is simply an unsubstantiated conviction, a blind conjecture. It is not scientific fact. Rather, it is pure faith.

Evolution's second foundational belief is that diverse species developed from a common ancestor. This premise is inherent in the word "evolution" itself, and involves the idea of living things changing from what they were into something altogether different. Simple organisms are said to have changed by chance into creatures much more sophisticated and complex. Some evolutionists argue that these changes were gradual, while others contend that they were sudden. But either way, evolution rests on the belief that all life has a common origin—that groups and species which are quite separate today (horses and hens, giraffes and glow-worms) originally had the same ancestor.

This premise, too, cannot be verified by science. Evolutionists believe that simple-to-complex species-change happened, and they cite circumstantial evidence to justify their belief—but they cannot prove that it happened, nor can they agree on how it might have happened. And while there is evidence that change can occur within a family (rock pigeons have been bred into racing and show pigeons), there is no verifiable evidence that change can (or did) occur across the families (pigeons have not been bred into parrots, let alone penguins or eagles).

If they are to be accepted at all, the two major premises of evolution must be accepted by faith. Of course, anyone is at liberty to believe that life can or did arise of its own volition from lifeless substances, and that simple organisms changed unaided into complex ones. But no one ought to think that science requires such a belief.

Evolution's major premises are faith assumptions, unproven and unprovable by science. Consequently, those who accept the evolutionary theory are acting on faith, while those who reject it are not rejecting science.

Is evolution compatible with creation?

Evolution, creation—both are faith positions, depending on premises that cannot be tested by science. So, as there is no conflict between fact and faith, there is no necessity to integrate the two positions. But can evolution and creation be integrated, nonetheless? Are the two faiths compatible or not? Can we believe a combination of both or should we choose one against the other?

Theistic evolutionists maintain that the two are compatible and can be combined. Motivated by the idea that evolution is scientific, and concerned to reconcile religion to science, they maintain that God created through the evolutionary process. There are many variations of this belief. For example, some theistic evolutionists believe that God started things off, then stepped back and allowed them to take their own evolutionary course. Others believe that God actually guided the evolutionary process. Still others postulate that God intervened in the evolutionary process to give man a soul. The common and crucial factor, however, is that evolution is the process by which God created the universe and all life.

Unfortunately, regardless of how it is argued, theistic evolution is a self-contradiction. It defies logic to say that God created through the evolutionary process.

To begin with, evolution is a naturalistic theory, attributing the origin of life to natural causes. By contrast, creation is a supernaturalistic theory, attributing the origin of life to supernatural causes. Naturalism maintains that nothing exists but matter, while supernaturalism maintains that there is also a spiritual component to the universe.

It is impossible to reconcile a view that there is only matter with a view that there is also spirit. Logically, a naturalistic theory cannot admit the supernatural

192

without ceasing to be naturalistic. The evolutionary theory ceases to be a naturalistic theory the moment God is introduced to it. If God started life off, or guided the development of the species, or intervened to give man a soul—if he did anything at all, then the evolutionary theory has failed in its attempt to explain the origin and development of life in purely natural, non-spiritual terms. Regardless of where or how they introduce the supernatural, theistic evolutionists destroy both the foundation and the intention of evolution.

In a similar vein, it is illogical to claim that God created via the evolutionary process because the concepts "God created" and "evolutionary process" cancel each other out. "God created" implies that life originated and/or developed according to the power and purpose of a supreme Being. By contrast, "evolutionary process" implies that life originated and developed according to spontaneous and random events. In short, "God created" involves order and purpose, while "evolutionary process" involves chaos and chance. The two concepts contradict each other utterly.

Also, the evolutionary process, being a natural process, is free from outside (supernatural) interference. It is self-contained. Hence, to say that God created via the evolutionary process is to say that God used a process in which he was not involved. It is to say that he created through a sequence of events that he neither initiated nor directed. This is illogical.

Even if theistic evolution were conceptually plausible, it would not be philosophically acceptable to most evolutionists, because they object to any hint of the supernatural. They value the evolutionary theory precisely because it allows them to explain matters without reference to God. Julian Huxley expressed the essential atheism of evolution when he wrote triumphantly: "The time is ripe for the dethronement of gods from their dominant position in our interpretation of destiny, in favour of a naturalistic type of belief-system. The supernatural is being swept out of the universe in the flood of new knowledge of what is natural."[3] Dethroning God and sweeping him out of the universe is evolution's triumph. Theistic evolutionists will get no thanks for trying to sneak him back in.

Evolution and creation are mutually exclusive worldviews. They cancel one another out at every point. Attempts to combine them arise from ignorance and result in absurdity.

Is evolution consistent with reality?

If evolution and creation are not compatible, then we must choose between them. But which faith is more reasonable? Which one best fits reality as we know it?

Reason favours creation in three significant ways.

The complexity of life is one reason to believe in a Creator. The life of even a single cell is so complicated that it beggars the imagination. One component of a living cell, for example, is protein. A protein molecule contains thousands of atoms arranged in intricate patterns. Sir Fred Hoyle, a British scientist who won the Nobel Prize for astronomy, has claimed that a simple functioning protein molecule is in itself sufficient to prove that evolution, which he once believed, is "nonsense of a high order". According to Sir Fred Hoyle's calculations, the odds against a single protein molecule originating by chance are the same as if you filled the solar system shoulder to shoulder with blind people, gave them each a scrambled Rubik's cube, then expected them all to get the right solution at the same time.[4] Yet evolutionists believe that not only proteins but also cells, and not only cells but also organs, and not only organs but also complete animals, arose by chance. To alleviate the absurdity of this notion, they speak of vast periods of time, as if time in and of itself possessed some life-giving magic. However, with or without billions of years, chance cannot explain the complexity of life. But creation can. A belief that life is the product of design is perfectly in keeping with both reality and reason.

The diversity of life is another reason to believe in a Creator. Living things are remarkably different from one another. Certainly, they are alike in various ways, sometimes notably so. Monkeys, orangutans, chimpanzees, gorillas and humans, for example, have similar limbs, hands and heads. Evolutionists cite these similarities as proof of a common ancestor. Creationists reply that they point to a common Creator. However, what matters are not the similarities, but the dissimilarities. And evolution has no plausible explanation for these. How can protein molecules and genetic materials be so vastly different from one organism to another? How can their biological structures and instinctual behaviours vary so strikingly? If all living things evolved from one original life-form, who can explain the enormous differences between the gills of a fish and the lungs of a porpoise, the hoof of a sheep and the paw of a dog, the

194

beak of an eagle and the bill of a finch, the nose of a shrew and the trunk of an elephant, the antennae of a moth and the radar of a bat, the fur of a rabbit and the feathers of a dove? Evolutionists consider that tens of thousands of happy coincidences occurred in sequence over time to produce each of these differences. They believe in miracle upon miracle without a God to perform them. Such faith is blind, illogical, irrational. It is much more reasonable to believe that the diversity of living things arises from the fact that almighty God made them "after their kind."[5]

The difference between human and animal life is yet another reason to believe in a Creator. There is a non-biological component to human beings that does not exist in other creatures. The magnitude of this difference can be seen, for example, in the relationship between a man and a dog. A man can teach a dog to fetch the newspaper, but he can never teach it to read the news. He can teach it not to bite the postman, but he can never teach it why it is wrong to bite him. He can teach it to howl while he sings, but he can never teach it to see the humour in the situation. He can teach it not to dig up the flowers, but he can never teach it to admire them. He can teach it to round up the sheep, but he can never teach it the purpose behind the round-up. He can teach it to lead a blind person, but he can never teach it to aspire to be a guide dog. Between a man and a dog, as between all humans and all animals, there is a spiritual gap as vast as the universe.

Alone among all earthly creatures, human beings have the ability to reason, talk, philosophise, sympathise, laugh, imagine, initiate, evaluate, admire, aspire, regret, repent, wonder and worship. These abilities have no counterpart in nature. They are spiritual—and therefore inexplicable in naturalistic terms. Consequently, evolutionists attempt to explain them by explaining them away. They deny that humans are more than biological organisms, and insist that there is no significant difference between humans and animals. Creationists, however, have a reasonable explanation for the spiritual nature of human beings—namely, that God made humans in his own likeness, giving them an eternal soul. The unique moral, emotional, intellectual and volitional characteristics and capacities of humans come from, and point to, God.

Evolution is not a reasonable faith. Its explanations for reality as we know it are implausible. Creation, on the other hand, offers sensible explanations for the complexity of life, the diversity of life forms, and the differences between humans and animals.

Conclusion

Is evolution based on science? Is it compatible with creation? Is it consistent with reality? The answer to each of these questions is, No! When people understand this they are freed from the pressure to accommodate the evolutionary theory. Then Christians can have confidence in the creation teaching of the Bible and non-Christians can begin to see their need to entrust themselves to a faithful Creator.

Christians and Politics

Politics is the "science and art of government" (*Oxford Dictionary*). Any person or party who tries to win government and/or keep government is involved in politics. So, too, is anyone who tries to influence the appointment of a government and/or the policies of a government.

The question for Christians is: Should we be involved in politics? Can political action and Christian devotion mix? Is it possible to participate in the art of government while maintaining a state of integrity? In short, may the people of God participate in the politics of men—and if so, to what end and by what means?

Politics in perspective

Christians involved in, or concerned about, political affairs can take some guidance from Hebrews 13:14: "here we have no lasting city, but we seek the city which is to come." This statement helps us to keep our political concerns in balance. It reminds us of four truths.

Firstly, we are mortal. We will not live in this world forever. There will come a time when we must meet our Creator, who will judge us not on our affiliation with a political party but on our affiliation with the risen Christ.

Secondly, all human ideologies and institutions are transient, fleeting. Therefore, we should not value earthly philosophies and institutions above their worth. We should not attribute to them an importance their impermanence belies. We should not act as if political and social structures and programmes are our first and final concern.

Thirdly, our future is in the Otherworld. The writer to the Hebrews says of Abraham, Sarah, Isaac and Jacob, "These all died in faith ... having acknowledged that they were strangers and exiles on the earth. For people who speak thus make it clear that they are seeking a homeland" (11:13-14). As Christians, we "desire a better country, that is, a heavenly one" (11:16). Indeed, we not only desire, we already belong to, that better country. For in addition to our worldly citizenship, we "are fellow citizens with the saints and members of the household of God" (Eph 2:19).

Fourthly, our allegiance is to the King of kings and our confidence is in him. As Christians, we should not be political partisans. Our political support should always be critical and conditioned by the requirements of righteousness as revealed in God's word. We should not blindly adhere to any party or ideology. We should not wholly trust anyone but God. We know the wisdom of the psalmist's words: "It is better to take refuge in the Lord than to put confidence in man. It is better to take refuge in the Lord than to put confidence in princes" (Ps 118:8-9).

We are going to die; our institutions will not last; our home is in Heaven; we dare not fully trust any ruler but God: these four observations seem to argue against Christian involvement in political affairs. But in fact they do not. They merely help us to keep politics in perspective.

For paradoxically, behind mortality we glimpse eternity and behind transience we glimpse permanence. Hence, when we understand the fleeting nature of life we come to value human endeavours both less and more. Less, because we know they will not last in their present form. More, because we know they will have eternal consequences. What we do now, whether good or ill, matters. It matters right now and on into eternity.

Christians are required to love God first; but they cannot love him without loving their neighbour, who is made in his image. Christians are required to set their desire on things above; but they cannot do this unless they show due concern for things below. A saving faith always results in a serving life; and that service is often directed to God via our fellow man.

The provision of good government is one way we may serve both God and man. Therefore it is not only acceptable but also necessary for Christians to be concerned with the political affairs of the nation and the world.

A political parable

There is a parable in the book of Judges (9:8-15) that has political significance for God's people:

The trees once went forth to anoint a king over them; and they said to the olive tree, "Reign over us." But the olive tree said to them, "Shall I leave my fatness, by which gods and men are honoured, and go to sway over the trees?" And the trees said to the fig tree, "Come you, and reign over us." But the fig tree said to them, "Shall I leave my sweetness and my good fruit, and go to sway over the trees?" And the trees said to the vine, "Come you, and reign over us." But the vine said to them, "Shall I leave my wine which cheers gods and men, and go to sway over the trees?" Then all the trees said to the bramble, "Come you, and reign over us." And the bramble said to the trees, "If in good faith you are anointing me king over you, then come and take refuge in my shade; but if not, let fire come out of the bramble and devour the cedars of Lebanon."

Whatever this parable originally meant, it certainly confirms the maxim that "All it takes for evil to flourish is for good men to do nothing."

It is significant that the trees first approached three good and noble trees to "sway over" them. However, the olive, the fig and the vine considered politics to be either disreputable or diversionary: it is an undignified pursuit, or, at best, an unimportant one. These noble trees had, so they thought, better things to do. As a last resort, the trees petitioned the bramble; and this worthless bush became king by default.

"Take refuge in my shade", said the bramble to the trees; "but if not, let fire come out of the bramble and devour the cedars of Lebanon." We may be sure that the trees could no more take refuge in the bramble's shade than they could stop the fire coming from it to consume them. And we may be sure, too, that when the fire came, the olive, the fig, and the vine were not spared.

Should the fire of bad government consume our nation, would Christians escape the flames? And even if we had some fire-proof ark, would we be justified in fleeing to it when, with our help, the fire could be quenched or confined?

If we want enduring good government, we need to be involved in the political process. But before we can do this, we need to establish our political objectives.

Key political goals

What ought to be the political goals of the people of God in the present age? Several objectives come readily to mind.

Solomon tells us that "Righteousness exalts a nation" (Prov 14:34). A chief aim, then, is *righteousness*. What we mean by this is that we will strive to ensure that our personal and national behaviour corresponds with the commands and character of God. Whether individual or collective, we want our actions to be informed by "rightwiseness".

In order to ensure that righteousness is respected in our nation, Christians should guard against the adoption and implementation of wrong policies by our government. Our second objective, then, is *vigilance*. We should be the nation's watchdogs. We should bark and bite every time our government tries to open the gate to unrighteousness.

If we are to be effective watchdogs, we should not allow ourselves to be chained to any political organisation. Hence, our third objective is *independence*. We should strive to act in the political arena without becoming party-political. We do not want to place undue faith in any government or party. We want to be honest in matters of criticism or praise. We may support one party as "better than" (or "not as bad as") another but we will never support it uncritically.

Our integrity depends upon our independence, and so too does the way we are called to live. The apostle Paul instructs us to pray for our government in order "that we may lead a quiet and peaceable life" (I Tim 2:1-2). We want to be left alone. We do not want the government to do for us things we can and should do for ourselves. We want to minimise government interference in personal, family and church life so that we can get on with our daily affairs in a godly manner.

Our fourth objective is *conservation*. We must conserve, preserve, defend our democratic institutions. Because it provides both the freedom to expose lies and the mechanism to control corruption, constitutional parliamentary democracy (involving separation of powers, rule of law, accountability of governments, freedom of expression and respect for human rights) is one of the best secular servants of righteousness known to man. In our fallen world, democracy preserves justice, freedom, truth and prosperity as no other political system.

Democracy embodies a view of human nature identical to that of

Christianity—namely, that men and women are corrupt. Consequently, whether they are kings or commoners, they must be restrained. Democracy works on the principle that no person or group of persons may be trusted with excessive power. It works by providing a system of checks and balances on government. Democracy is the art of distrust—and that is why Christians can tentatively trust it.

Righteousness, vigilance, independence, conservation: for the Christian, these are prime political goals. Interestingly, they are also the means by which the goals are to be achieved.

Proposals for political action

There are several ways that Christians can be involved in the political process. Before mentioning these, however, it is worth noting a foundational matter.

In a democracy the rights of citizenship belong to Christians as much as to anyone else and it is not improper for us to use those rights. Paul demonstrates this on several occasions. In Acts 16:37 he asserts his rights as a Roman citizen to extract an apology from the authorities for false imprisonment. In Acts 22:25 he asserts his rights as a Roman citizen to avoid a scourging. In Acts 25:11 he asserts his rights as a Roman citizen to appeal to Caesar. Being a Christian did not strip Paul of his rights as a citizen, nor did it prevent him from claiming those rights. The same is true today for Christians living in a democracy like Australia. This means that (among other things) we have a right to get involved in the political process.

This involvement can take three forms.

Influence on the government: One way to get involved in the political process is to attempt to influence government policies. No less than other citizens, Christians have a right to hold and to express distinctive views—and we have a right to try to influence our governments in order to bring about the implementation of those views. We can exert influence by expressing our views to members of parliament by phone or letter or email. We can also exert influence by attending rallies, signing petitions and writing letters to newspapers—and by encouraging others to do likewise.

Selection of the government: Another way to get involved in the political process is to cast a vote with care at election time. Political parties vary in the degree to which they sympathise with Christian values, so we need to find and vote for the most sympathetic. Ways to evaluate the various parties include reading their platforms, heeding the media statements by their leaders, and noting the voting patterns of their parliamentarians. A little care before voting can save a lot of care afterwards. Certainly, it is better to elect a sympathetic government than to lobby a hostile one.

Entrance to the government: Yet another way to get involved in the political process is to run for parliament. In a democracy, Christians, too, may endeavour to enter parliament through the electoral process. There are two main methods of doing this. One is to join a mainstream political party that is not hostile to Christian values. The other is to join a Christian political party that actively promotes Christian values. Either course of action is potentially useful.

Of course, running for parliament is not the only reason for joining a political party. Christians may take up membership in order to help the party frame good policies, select good candidates and run successful election campaigns.

Joining a mainstream political party poses some dangers. The Christian party member may be tempted either to forsake what is right for what is expedient or to place loyalty to the party above loyalty to the Lord. But these dangers may be braved by Christians who genuinely seek to honour the Lord through political action.

The right to engage in the political process involves a responsibility to educate ourselves in political realities. We need to keep abreast of current affairs. We need to guard against media bias. We need to develop a biblical mindset and learn how to apply biblical principles to government policies. And we need to persevere in doing these things, confident that the Lord will use our efforts for his purposes.

The prophet Isaiah states: "When the enemy shall come in like a flood, the Spirit of the Lord shall lift up a standard against him" (59:19, AV). Yes. And the wonder of it is that, when we yield ourselves to his control, *we* are the standard the Spirit lifts up.

Biblical and Social Justice Views on Poverty and the Poor

"Social justice" was traditionally the rallying cry of the politically left and the theologically liberal. But in recent years it has been increasingly taken up by evangelical, conservative and Bible-believing Christians; and it is increasingly drawing these Christians into the folds of leftwing politics and liberal theology.

The popularity of social justice among Christians has soared in the past few decades largely because the political parties of the left have sought to use it to counter the concerns and influence of conservative Christians on "moral" issues such as abortion, pornography, prostitution and homosexuality. Indeed, some evangelicals were persuaded to support the Labor Party in the 2007 federal election primarily on the grounds of Mr Rudd's arguments that social justice ought to be more important to Christians than personal morality.

Two quotations from two champions of social justice will help to focus our understanding of what the social justice position involves. The first is from Jim Wallis, a social justice campaigner and author in the United States. The second is from Kevin Rudd, the former Prime Minister of Australia.

In an interview about his book, *God's Politics: Why the Right Gets It Wrong and the Left Doesn't Get It*, Jim Wallis made these comments:

> The Right is comfortable with the language of religion, values, God talk. So much so that they sometimes claim to own that territory. Or own God. But then they narrow everything down to one or two issues: abortion and gay marriage.
>
> I am an evangelical Christian, and I can't ignore thousands of

verses in the Bible on [another] subject, which is poverty. I say at every stop, "Fighting poverty's a moral value, too."[1]

Kevin Rudd made similar statements in his essay, "Faith and Politics". Midway through the essay he mentions and mocks four ways that modern Christians supposedly engage in politics. The second is:

> *Vote for me because I'm Christian, and because I have a defined set of views on a narrowly defined set of questions concerning sexual morality.* Regrettably, this model has an increasing number of supporters within the broader Christian community. Such supporters tend to read down, rather than read up, the ethical teachings of the New Testament, producing a narrow tick-the-box approach to passing a so-called Christian morals test. These tests tend to emphasise questions of sexuality and sexual behaviour. I see very little evidence that this pre-occupation with sexual morality is consistent with the spirit and content of the Gospels.[2]

Wallis and Rudd share a "social justice" or "social gospel" or "Christian socialist" worldview. From their comments quoted above, it is evident that both men consider "social" issues such as poverty to be far more important than "personal" issues such as abortion and homosexuality. Indeed, they seem quite reluctant to credit matters of sexual morality with any importance at all. And they are peeved by Christians who do attribute importance to such issues. These narrow- and feeble-minded Christians of "the religious Right", they would have us believe, are gagging at gnats while scoffing down camels.

In this brief essay, I do not propose to deal with the false notions that poverty can be separated from sexual morality, or that moral issues are relatively unimportant, or that a concern for them precludes a concern for poverty and the poor. My focus is on those aspects of the biblical teaching about poverty that Christian advocates of social justice ignore, aspects that balance the biblical view and counterbalance, if not countermand, the social justice view.

While advocates of social justice claim to be aware of "thousands of verses" in the Bible on poverty, they are quite selective about the verses they quote. They make no mention, for example, of the many Bible verses that lay the blame for poverty at the feet of the poor.

And yes, the Bible does indeed teach that, in some circumstances, the poor are responsible for their own poverty. In this essay, I want to draw attention to this neglected biblical teaching about poverty and the poor.

But note at the outset that I have said *"in some circumstances"* the poor, according to the Bible, are to blame for their plight. I am well aware that the Bible envisages other circumstances in which the poor are poor through no fault of their own. And I am well aware that the Bible defends—and exhorts the righteous to defend—such people. There is no need for thousands of verses to establish this fact. One will do: "Whoever oppresses a poor man insults his Maker, but he who is generous to the needy honours him" (Prov 14:31).

I do not claim that the passages I am about to quote represent the sum total of the Bible's teaching about poverty and the poor. I merely claim that they represent an important aspect of the Bible's teaching, an aspect that social justice advocates gloss over. And by evading this teaching, they distort the biblical position on the origin of poverty, the solution to poverty, and the nature of the poor.

The Bible plainly and emphatically teaches that some instances of poverty are caused by the behaviour of the impoverished people concerned. For example:

People can bring poverty on themselves by being lazy: "A slack hand causes poverty, but the hand of the diligent makes rich" (Prov 10:4). This statement is notable for its identification of the cause not only of poverty, but also of wealth. Social justice advocates would have us believe that, in the main, the poor are poor because they are exploited by the rich and the rich are rich because they exploit the poor. Sometimes, no doubt, this is true. But the Bible will not allow that it is the whole truth.

There are repeated warnings in Prov about the link between laziness and poverty. Here are a few: "The sluggard does not plough in the autumn; he will seek at harvest and have nothing" (Prov 20:4). "Love not sleep, lest you come to poverty; open your eyes, and you will have plenty of bread" (Prov 20:13). "The desire of the sluggard kills him, for his hands refuse to labour" (Prov 21:25). "A little sleep, a little slumber, a little folding of the hands to rest, and poverty will come upon you like a robber, and want like an armed man" (Prov 24:33-34; cf 6:6-11 & 19:15).

People can bring poverty on themselves by pursuing a life of pleasure: "Whoever loves pleasure will be a poor man; he who loves wine and oil will not be rich" (Prov 21:17).

People can bring poverty on themselves through poor stewardship of their resources, through extravagance and wastefulness: "Precious treasure and oil are in a wise man's dwelling, but a foolish man devours it" (Prov 21:20).

People can bring poverty on themselves by unwise generosity and misguided goodwill: "Be not one of those who give pledges, who put up security for debts. If you have nothing with which to pay, why should your bed be taken from under you" (Prov 22:26-27; *cf* 6:1-5)?

People can bring poverty on themselves by refusing to follow wise counsel, but instead defiantly do as they please: "Poverty and disgrace come to him who ignores instruction, but whoever heeds reproof is honoured" (Prov 13:18).

People can bring poverty on themselves through greed, devising or joining rash schemes to get rich: "A faithful man will abound with blessings, but whoever hastens to be rich will not go unpunished" (Prov 28:20; cf 28:22). "The plans of the diligent lead surely to abundance, but everyone who is hasty comes only to poverty" (Prov 21:5).

People can bring poverty on themselves by spending their time on useless pastimes: "Whoever works his land will have plenty of bread, but he who follows worthless pursuits will have plenty of poverty" (Prov 28:19; cf 12:11).

People can bring poverty on themselves by keeping bad company: "Be not among drunkards or among gluttonous eaters of meat, for the drunkard and the glutton will come to poverty, and slumber will clothe them with rags" (Prov 23:20-21).

People can bring poverty on themselves by engaging in sexual immorality: "these commands are a lamp … keeping you from the immoral woman … Do not lust in your heart after her beauty or let her captivate you with her eyes, for the prostitute reduces you to a loaf of bread, and the adulteress preys upon your very life" (Prov 6:20-26; cf 5:4-14).

According to the Bible, then, the poor are sometimes poor because of their own wrong choices and actions. Hedonism, extravagance, foolishness, drunkenness, gluttony, sexual immorality, laziness, bad company—these are causes of poverty that the advocates of social justice never mention. And these are causes of poverty that, in the first instance, no one but the poor themselves can do anything about. For if it is true that poverty is sometimes caused by the moral failings of the poor, then it is also true that the solution to those instances of poverty is not primarily institutional and social but personal and moral. The solution has to do with the poor taking personal responsibility for their actions and embarking upon personal reform. This is something that advocates of social justice are either unable to understand or unwilling to acknowledge.

One of the unforeseen results of the gospel revivals in England and Wales in the eighteenth and nineteenth centuries was a general increase in prosperity and wellbeing in the lives of those who were converted. For spiritual conversion resulted in moral reformation, which in turn resulted in the abandonment of behaviours that produce poverty. For example, the men who became Christians gave up drinking alcohol and that alone meant more money was available for the needs of their families. But other benefits flowed from their abstinence. The end of drinking meant an end to drunkenness, which in turn put an end to brawling and to hangovers, which in turn put an end to injury and days missed at work, which in turn put more money the pockets of the men and their families. And so on.

The Bible has other things to say about poverty and the poor that are in conflict with much socialist and social justice thinking. For example, it instructs us not to show favouritism to the poor in matters of justice: "You shall not fall in with the many to do evil ... nor shall you be partial to a poor man in his lawsuit" (Exod 23:2-3). Thanks to the influence of the social justice movement, many people in the West are highly prejudiced in favour of the poor (and those deemed to be poor), and will make any excuse for them and express any demand on their behalf. But fair-minded people should not "fall in with the many" in this regard. Again, the Bible instructs: "You shall not be partial in judgment. You shall hear the small and the great alike. You shall not be intimidated by anyone, for the judgment is God's" (Deut 1:17). And yet again: "You shall do no injustice in court. You shall not be partial to the poor or defer to the great, but in righteousness shall you judge your neighbour" (Lev 19:15). Thankfully, most people in our society believe it is wrong to favour the rich; but, sadly, few people believe it is wrong to favour the poor. However, the Bible insists that it is unjust to side with a man simply because he is poor or to side against a man simply because he is rich.

The Bible also notes that the poor can themselves be oppressors of the poor: "A poor man who oppresses the poor is a beating rain that leaves no food" (Prov 28:3).

Albeit tangentially, Jesus affirms this truth in his parable about forgiveness, in which he compares the kingdom of heaven "to a king who wished to settle accounts with his servants". The King forgave the debt of a servant who owed the enormous sum of 10,000 talents. "But when that same servant went out, he found one of his fellow servants who owed him a hundred denarii, and seizing him, he began to choke him, saying, 'Pay what you owe.'" When this second servant could not pay, the first servant "put him in prison until he should pay the debt" (Matt 18:23-35). Given the chance, the poor sometimes oppress their fellow poor. Such is the fallen nature of man—not the fallen nature of rich men only, but of poor men, too.

Jesus' parable in Matthew 18 alerts us to several important truths about the rich, the poor and the payment of debts.

Firstly, wealth and exploitation are not necessarily linked. The rich are not, simply because they are rich, automatically wicked and oppressive. Wealth and power can be, and often are, justly obtained and justly exercised. Certainly, Jesus thinks highly enough of the rich and powerful king to liken him and his actions to "the kingdom of heaven".

Secondly, the rich have a right to receive back the money that they lend, as do the poor. The king did no wrong when he decided to settle his accounts with the servant. The servant had borrowed the king's money and he was required to pay it back. The repayment of debt is a matter of justice—justice for the one who owns the money and has lent it on agreed terms.

Thirdly, when the rich forgive debt, it is not an example of social justice. It is, in fact, an example of social mercy. When the king forgave the servant his debt, he was not being just, he was being merciful. For mercy's sake, he gave up his just claim and freed the servant of his debt. The servant who was unable to repay his debt was the recipient not of justice but of mercy. Justice is about getting what we deserve. Mercy, on the other hand, is about not getting what we deserve.

Fourthly, the behaviour of the first servant towards the second servant reveals that the poor are at heart no different from the rich. The poor are not nobler than the rich. In the main, the poor want the same thing as the rich—riches! They are as likely (or unlikely) to oppress someone beneath them as they are likely (or unlikely) to be oppressed by someone above them. Essentially, they do not have less inclination but less opportunity to engage in certain types of evil.

The passages of scripture cited above present a very different view of poverty and the poor from the social justice view. They round out the biblical position by showing that sometimes the poor are responsible for their own poverty because of their moral failings and/or their mistreatment of one another. They show that the poor are not always and only innocent victims of circumstance and oppression.

Of course, people can be poor—and many are poor—through no fault of their own. There are many implicit and explicit acknowledgements of this in the Bible. People can be poor because they are born into poor circumstances and lack the opportunity to change those circumstances. They can be poor because of natural disasters or ill health or injury. They can be poor because they do not have and cannot get employment or because they have never had the opportunity to obtain an education. And, of course, they can be poor because they have been cheated or intimidated or abused in some other way. Some of these causes of poverty are nobody's fault, while some of them are other people's fault.

However, advocates of social justice tend to gloss over the causes of poverty that are nobody's fault, and they likewise tend to gloss over the causes of poverty that are the poor person's fault. Instead, they focus on the causes of poverty that are (or that they believe are) the fault of the rich and powerful. In the process, they give the impression that the poor are poor always and only because they have been exploited and oppressed. (And the rich, powerful exploiters are generally supposed to be white, Western persons, corporations and nations. Even when a black dictator impoverishes and terrorises his own black people in Africa, advocates of social justice will find a white capitalist imperialist under the bed somewhere.) Furthermore, they manage to imply that anyone in the West (apart from themselves) who is not living in poverty is somehow implicated in the plight of those who are. The Bible does not support such notions of collective guilt and class warfare.

None of this is an argument against helping the poor—even the poor who are poor by their own foolishness or wickedness. It is an argument against making the well-off feel that they have somehow wronged the poor simply by being well-off. It is an argument against making guilt the basis for helping the poor. It is an argument against encouraging the poor to have a sense of entitlement to the wealth of those who are not poor. It is an argument against encouraging the poor to feel that when they are helped they have merely gotten what they are owed. It is an argument against encouraging ingratitude and envy in the poor and guilt and shame in the not-poor. It is an argument against the condescending self-righteous notion that those in the West who do help the poor do so only because they have grudgingly faced up to their collective guilt and belatedly acquiesced to the dictates of social justice. It is an argument against confusing justice with mercy and thereby demanding as a right what should be entreated as a favour.

People who are well off (which means most people in the West) should help the poor. But they should do so from generosity, not guilt. They should do so not because justice demands it but because mercy implores it. In short, they should do so not because of, but in spite of, the spurious dogmas and demands of social justice.

REFERENCES

Inca Child Sacrifices
1. *The Bulletin*, 20 April 1999, p.96.

Believing the Bible: the Issue of Inerrancy
1. *The Battle For The Bible* (Zondervan, 1976), p.37.
2. *op cit*, p.34.
3. See John R.W. Stott's *The Bible: book for today* (Inter-Varsity Press, 1981), pp.36-52.
4. *Freedom, Authority & Scripture* (Inter-Varsity Press, 1981), p.16.
5. *op cit*, p.18.
6. *The Great Evangelical Disaster* (Kingsway Publications, 1985), p.57.

The Supreme Importance of the Unity of God
1. William Evans, *The Great Doctrines Of The Bible*, p. 26.
2. *Roland Enroth (ed), Evangelising the Cults, (Word Publishing, 1991), p. 85.*
3. *ELOHIM Journal*, Vol.4, No.5, October/November 1999.
4. *The West Australian*, "Today", 10 August 1999, p. 3.

The Question of Truth
1. David A. Noebel, *Understanding the Times* (Manitou springs, CO: Summit Press, Revised 2nd Edition, 2nd printing, 2008), p. 9.
2. *ibid*, p. 25.

When Christians Take Their Lives
1. The Rev Dr Allen Fleece, Principal of the Columbia Bible College (1953-1966), made a comment to this effect in a sermon that I heard on audio tape many years ago. Unfortunately, I cannot recall the particular message or the exact comment.
2. "There's not a Friend like the lowly Jesus" by Johnson Oatman Jr.

The Way of the Samurai

1. Yamamoto Tsunetomo, *Hagakure: The Book of the Samurai*, translated by William Scott Wilson (Tokyo: Kodansha International, 1979; rpt. 1983).

Marriage According to Scripture

1. Although I am unable to cite a reference, I believe I gained this insight from something C. S. Lewis wrote.

The Origin of Fatherhood

1. Dorothy Lenthall, "Whose baby am I?", *The West Australian*, "Big Weekend", 15 July 1995, p.5.

2. David Blankenhorn, *Fatherless America* (Basic Books, 1995); part of chapter 6, quoted in *The Australian Family*, Vol.16, No.2, July 1995.

3. E.K. Simpson and F.F. Bruce, *Commentary on the Epistles to the Ephesians and Colossians* (Grand Rapids: Eerdmans, 1957; rpt 1975), p.76.

4. John R.W. Stott, *The Message of Ephesians* (Leicester: Inter-Varsity Press, 1984; rpt 1991), p.134.

The First Duty of Fatherhood

1. Anne Manne, "A Reflection upon Re-entering the World", *Quadrant*, June 1994.

2. Anne Manne, "Children in the New World Order", *Quadrant*, June 1995.

3. Quoted by Ray O'Sullivan, "The Debate - Part 2", *Endeavour Forum*, No.84, September 1996, p.13.

In Defence of the Unborn

1. *Pelican*, a publication of the Guild of Undergraduates, University of Western Australia, April 1989.

2. Carol Everett, *The Scarlet Lady*, Brentwood, Tennessee: Wolgemuth & Hyatt, 1991.

If people were dogs and other false arguments for euthanasia

1. Paul van Reyk, *Choosing to Die: A booklet for people thinking about euthanasia and for those asked to assist* (AIDS Council of New South Wales, 1994), p.11.

2. "Holland shows how euthanasia leads to active killing", *News Weekly*, 25 February 1995, p.6.

3. "Euthanasia in Holland", *Right to Life News*, March 1995, p.3.

4. "Holland shows how euthanasia leads to active killing", *op. cit.*

5. *Reader's Digest*, February 1998.

212

1. "Encounter" programme, ABC Radio National, 17 October 1993. Available on cassette tape from ABC Radio Tape Sales.

2. "Euthanasia in Holland", *op. cit.*

3. Paul van Reyk, *op. cit.*, pp.7, 12-13.

A Biblical Perspective on Prostitution

1. *The West Australian*, "Classified Liftout", 13 December 1997, pp.65-66.

2. Linda, interviewed by Dwight Randall, "Prostitution in Perth", Life Ministries Current Issues Paper, January 1998.

Prostitution and Social Justice

1. Advertisement, personal columns, *The West Australian*, 19 August 1998, p.101.

2. "The Warsaw Proposition", *On Being*, April 1986, p.50.

3. *The West Australian*, 19 August 1998, p.100.

4. "Girls clamour to join brothels", *Western Mail*, 9 October 1987, p.1.

How Pornography Harms Us

1. These testimonies can be read in *Pornography's Victims*, edited by Phyllis Schlafly (Illinios: Crossway Books, 1987). *Pornography's Victims* is a collection of excerpts from the Official Transcript of Proceedings before the Attorney General's Commission on Pornography in the United States in 1985-1986.

2. Ted Bundy, interviewed by Dr James Dobson on the video *Pornography: Addictive, Progressive and Deadly* (Focus on the Family Films, 1994).

Obsessed with Sex?

1. *The West Australian*, 9 December 2000, p.1.

How Green Is God

1. See, for example, my book *Birds in Mind: Australian Nature Poems* (Wombat Books, 2009). This collection contains over 200 nature poems, many of them selected from my other books.

2. "How Green is God?" is based on my earlier, shorter essay, "The Greenness of God".

3. See Acts 14:15; Jeremiah 10:12; Psalm 104:24-25; Revelation 4:11.

4. "How Man Began", *Time*, 14 March, 1994, p.55.

Sympathy for a Shark

1. *The West Australian*, 8 November 2000.

Evolution?

1. Australian Academy of Science, *Biological Science: the web of life* (Canberra: Australian Academy of Science, 1967; reprinted 1969), p.547. This book was designed for senior students and was my biology text at high school.
2. *ibid*, p.672.
3. Julian Huxley, *Religion Without Revelation* (London: Max Parrish, 1957), p.62.
4. Sir Fred Hoyle, "The Big Bang in Astronomy," *New Scientist*, Vol.92, No.1280, 19 November 1981, p.527.
5. *The Holy Bible*, Genesis 1.

Biblical and Social Justice Perspectives on Poverty and the Poor

1. "God's Politics: An Interview with Jim Wallis", Michal Lumsden (interviewer), MotherJones.com, 10 March 2005.
2. Kevin Rudd, "Faith and Politics", *The Monthly*, October 2006.

ACKNOWLEDGEMENTS

All of the essays in this collection have been publish by Life Ministries Inc (Nollamara, WA, Australia) in the organisation's quarterly magazine, *Life News*, or as stand-alone pamphlets in the ministry's Life Pamphlets series. Most of the essays (often with revisions) have also been published in various magazines and newspapers.

Becoming a Christian — Pamphlet, Life Ministries, 1989; reprinted 2000, 2003, 2005 & 2007. *Challenge*, October 2003 (titled, "What's Christianity about?"). *Communication Broadcast* (George Galieh Evangelistic Crusades), 2000.

One for All — Pamphlet, Life Ministries, 2004; reprinted 2004 (twice), 2005, 2007 & 2011. *Challenge*, June 2004.

Sticky Tape Mechanic — *Challenge*, March 1996; February 2000. *Life News*, September 1996. *Australian Stories to Bless the Soul* (Sydney, Strand Publishing), 2007.

An Accurate Diagnosis — Pamphlet, Life Ministries, 2007; reprinted 2014. *Challenge*, September 1998 (titled, "A perfect cure"); February 2001 (titled, "The Cure"); September 2006. *Life News*, October 2001.

A Christmas Carol — Pamphlet, Life Ministries, 2000; reprinted 2003 & 2014. *The Briefing*, December 2002 (titled, "Something worth harking about"). *Challenge*, December 2003 (titled, "Worth harking about"). *New Life*, 4 December 2003. *Sydney Anglican Network*, 23 December 2007 (titled, "Christmas Carols: Something Worth Harking About").

An Easter Song — Pamphlet, Life Ministries, 2007; reprinted 2014 & 2018. *Challenge*, March 2008. *Challenge* (USA), Edition 8, 2009. *New Life*, 20 March 2008 (titled, "An Easter song – with eternal truth").

Inca Child Sacrifices — *The Briefing,* July 1999; *Challenge,* July 1999 & October 2007; August 1999; *Life News,* June 1999.

Believing the Bible: The Issue of Inerrancy — Pamphlet, Life Ministries, 1987; reprinted 1988 & 2013. *New Life,* 12 November 1987.

The Supreme Importance of the Unity of God — *Life News,* July 2016.

The Desirability of Sound Doctrine — Pamphlet, Life Ministries, 1990.

The Question of Truth — *Life News,* No. 112, April 2010.

Engraved on God's Hands — *Life News,* February 2009. *The Briefing,* July 2009.

When Christians Take Their Lives — Pamphlet, Life Ministries, 2013. *Life News,* October 2003. *New Life,* 15 February 2007.

Making Sense of Disaster — Pamphlet, Life Ministries, 2016. *Life News,* October 1999; January 2020. *New Life,* 28 October 1999. *The Briefing,* 17 May 2000. *Challenge,* September 1999; February 2005.

Choose the Right Counsellor — *Life News,* December 2020.

The Way of the Samurai — Pamphlet, Life Ministries, 2013. *Challenge,* August 2002. *Challenge* (New Zealand), No.16, 2002. *Today's Challenge* (South Africa), No.5, 2002.

Marriage According to Scripture — Pamphlet, Life Ministries, 1994; reprinted 2007. *Light,* May 1994 (extract titled "What Jesus said about marriage …"). *Marriage Works Magazine* (online), 21 January 2009.

The Origin of Fatherhood — Pamphlet, Life Ministries, 1996. *New Life,* 4 September 1997. *Future Trends: Understanding Tomorrow's World* (Mount Waverly, Vic: Teach All Nations Inc, 2005). *Abundant Life,* September 2009. *Life News,* February 2014.

The First Duty of Fatherhood — Pamphlet, Life Ministries, 1997. *The Briefing,* 13 August 1997. *Challenge,* September 1997. *New Life,* 2 October 1997. *Life News,* February 2018. *Abundant Life,* Winter 2018.

The High King's Watchmen — Pamphlet, Life Ministries, 1988; reprinted May 2015. *New Life,* 24 November 1988.

A Biblical Perspective on Abortion — Pamphlet, Life Ministries, 1998 (titled, "Abortion: A Biblical Perspective"). *Challenge,* in three parts, February-March-April 1993 (titled, "The value of human life: the abortion issue—Part 1", "Abortion: what reason infers: the abortion issue—Part 2" & "Abortion:

216

arguments against/for—Part 3"). *New Life*, in two parts, 25 June 1998 & 2 July 1998. *Salt Shakers*, May 1999 (titled, "Abortion: A Biblical Perspective"). *Life News*, July 2018.

In Defence of the Unborn — Pamphlet, Life Ministries, 1993; reprinted 1998. *The Horatian*, Spring 1994. *Salt Shakers*, in three parts, February-April 2005 (titled, "Arguments against abortion", parts 1-3). *New Life*, in three parts, 21 April, 28 April & 5 May 2005 (titled, "Arguments against abortion", parts 1-3). *Challenge*, in three parts, March-April-May 2005 (titled, "Arguments against abortion (part 1)", "The abortion debate (part 2)", "The abortion debate (part 3)"). *Life News*, in three parts, April, June, August 2005 (titled, "Arguments against abortion", parts 1-3). *Challenge* (India), June 2010.

If People Were Dogs and Other False Arguments for Euthanasia — Pamphlet, Life Ministries, 1995 (originally titled, "Euthanasia: A Dangerous Enthusiasm"); reprinted (with current title) 2007.

Mistaken Support for Euthanasia — *Challenge*, October 1996; August 2007; October 2009. *Life News*, June 1997; August 2007 (titled, "Misunderstandings about euthanasia"); July 2017. *New Life*, 5 July 2007

A Biblical Perspective on Prostitution — Pamphlet, Life Ministries, 1998; reprinted 2007. *Salt Shakers*, in two parts, April & May 1998. *Challenge*, in three parts, February, March & May 1998 (titled, "How should we view prostitution?", parts 1-3).

Prostitution and Social Justice — Pamphlet, Life Ministries, 1988 (twice) (originally titled, "Prostitution"); reprinted (with current title) 1998 & 2007. *Light*, August 1988 (except titled "Prostitution—what harm does it do?"). *Logos Journal*, August 1991 (titled, "Prostitution"). *APEX in the West*, May 1988 (excerpt titled, "Is Prostitution a Victimless Crime?"). *New Life*, 26 May 1988 (titled, "Prostitution—And the Liberalisation of Laws Concerning It!"). *Challenge*, May 1988.

How Pornography Harms Us — Pamphlet, Life Ministries, 1999 (originally titled "The violence of pornography"); reprinted (with current title) 2007. *Challenge*, in three parts, April-May-June 2000 (titled "The violence of pornography").

Obsessed with Sex? — *Life News*, April 2001. *Salt Shakers*, February 2002.

How Green is God? — Pamphlet, Life Ministries, 1994; reprinted 2014.

Trends 2001: A Twenty-First Century Primer on the Future (Melbourne: Trends 2100/ Harvest Bible College, 2001). *Future Trends: Understanding Tomorrow's World* (Mount Waverly, Vic: Teach All Nations Inc, 2005). An earlier, shorter version of this essay, titled "The Greenness of God", was published: *Challenge*, May 1991. *New Life*, 2 May 1991 (titled, "The Greening of God"). *Life News*, April 1992. *Creation Ex Nihilo*, December 1992. *Mar Thoma Messenger*, March 1993. *NCV Quarterly*, Spring 1993. *The Toodyay Herald*, 3 April 1992. *Pingelly Times*, 1993.

Sympathy for a Shark — *Life News*, December 2000; April 2017. *Salt Shakers*, February 2001.

Evolution? — Pamphlet, Life Ministries, 1994; reprinted 2005. *The Alternative*, April 1997 (extract titled "Is Evolution Consistent with Reality?"). *Challenge*, in three parts, February-March-April 1997 (titled "Is evolution based on science?", "Is evolution compatible with creation?" & "Is evolution consistent with reality?"); in three parts, May-June-July 2001 (titled, "Evolution and science?", "Compatibility?" & "Opposite views of reality"); in three parts, September-October- November 2005 (titled, "The design-evolution debate (part 1): Is evolution based on science?", "The design-evolution debate (part 2): Is evolution compatible with creation?" & "The design-evolution debate (part 3): Is evolution consistent with reality?"). *Trends 2001: A Twenty-First Century Primer on the Future* (Melbourne: Trends 2100/Harvest Bible College, 2001; titled, "Reflections on Evolution and Creation"). *Future Trends: Understanding Tomorrow's World* (Mount Waverly, Vic: Teach All Nations Inc, 2005; titled, "Reflections On Evolution"). *New Life*, in three parts, 6 October 2005, 13 October 2005 & 20 October 2005 (titled, "The design-evolution debate (part 1): Is evolution based on science?", "The design-evolution debate (part 2): Is evolution compatible with creation?" & "The design-evolution debate (part 3): Is evolution consistent with reality?"). *Life News*, in three parts, October 2005, December 2005 & February 2006. (The first section of "Evolution?" is based on an earlier essay, "Faith Verses Faith", published in: *Contact*, November 1984; September 1987. *New Life*, 11 April 1985. *Challenge*, May 1986 (titled, "Evolution Versus Creation Debate"). *News Weekly*, 16 September 1987 (titled, "The evolution debate: a matter of faith versus faith"). *The Australian Baptist*, 8 February 1989. *Logos Journal*, July 1989. *Life News*, October 1989. *Pingelly Times*, 1993. *The Toodyay Herald*, 8 May 1992.)

Christians and Politics — Pamphlet, Life Ministries, 2013. *Contact*, September 1986 (titled, "Politics and God's People"). *The Australian Baptist*, 24 June 1987 (titled, "Politics and Piety: Some Christian Considerations"). *The Link: Weekly Newsletter from the Reformed Church of Perth*, 4 October 1987 (titled, "Politics and Piety—Some Christian Considerations"). *Logos Journal*, October 1987 (titled, "Politics and Piety"). *Life News*, April 1987 (titled, "Politics and Piety—Some Christian Considerations"); October 2004 (titled, "Christians and politics").

Biblical and Social Justice Perspectives on Poverty and the Poor — *Life News*, September 2010 (titled, "The social justice deception (1): On poverty and scripture"). *Quadrant*, September 2021 (titled, "The Bible, Social Justice and the Poor").

Bible translations — The Bible translations used in this collection of essays are the *Revised Standard Version* and the *English Standard Version*.